EVERY PROPHECY ABOUT JESUS

EVERY PROPHECY ABOUT JESUS

JOHN F. WALVOORD

David C Cook®

transforming lives together

EVERY PROPHECY ABOUT JESUS
Published by David C Cook
4050 Lee Vance View
Colorado Springs, CO 80918 U.S.A.

David C Cook Distribution Canada
55 Woodslee Avenue, Paris, Ontario, Canada N3L 3E5

David C Cook U.K., Kingsway Communications
Eastbourne, East Sussex BN23 6NT, England

The graphic circle C logo is a registered trademark of David C Cook.

LCCN 2015960924
ISBN 978-0-7814-1403-6
eISBN 978-1-4347-1013-0

© 2016 John F. Walvoord
Material adapted from *Every Prophecy of the Bible* (formerly titled
Prophecy Knowledge Handbook) © 1990, 2011 John F. Walvoord,
published by David C Cook, ISBN 978-1-4347-0386-6.

The Team: Tim Peterson, Keith Wall, Amy Konyndyk,
Nick Lee, Jack Campbell, Susan Murdock
Cover Design: Jon Middel
Cover Photo: Thinkstock

Printed in the United States of America
First Edition 2016

1 2 3 4 5 6 7 8 9 10

012816

CONTENTS

THE ONE AND ONLY SAVIOR

Jesus is quite literally the center point on the timeline of human history. That is why we categorize years as either BC (before Christ) or AD (anno Domini, Latin for "in the year of our Lord"). What's more, Jesus is the central figure in all of eternity—the much-anticipated Messiah long before He arrived on earth, the world-changing teacher while He walked the earth, and the King of Kings, who will return to earth to take His followers to heaven to live with Him forever.

Among the countless momentous occurrences that have marked the history of mankind, undoubtedly the life, death, and resurrection of Jesus represent the most significant events of all time. For thousands of years, people eagerly waited for the arrival of the Messiah and prophets precisely predicted the details of His earthly entrance, existence, and exit. Those blessed to live after Christ's death and resurrection marvel at the hundreds of prophecies He has already fulfilled and anticipate with assurance the ones yet to be fulfilled.

For believers, Jesus is everything—the way of salvation, the source of strength, and the reason for hope. We shouldn't be surprised, then, that as God's plans have unfolded—and will continue to do so—Jesus is at the heart of it all. Indeed, biblical prophecy has always focused on Jesus. In the Old Testament, God's prophets pointed to a king who would lead and deliver His followers. Those prophets didn't realize, however, that the Messiah would come to earth twice—first as a suffering savior and second as a conquering king.

All the biblical prophecies serve a powerful purpose: to demonstrate that Christ is the Son of God, the one and only Savior. As Revelation 19:10 says, "The essence of prophecy is to give a clear witness for Jesus" (NLT). The truth of this verse is certainly confirmed in the pages of Scripture. The Old Testament contains many passages about the Messiah—all prophecies Jesus Christ fulfilled. For instance, the crucifixion of Jesus was foretold in Psalm 22:16–18 a thousand years before Christ's birth, long before this method of execution was even practiced. Moreover, scholars affirm that Jesus fulfilled more than three hundred prophetic scriptures.

The book you hold in your hands presents the prophecies pertaining to Jesus that have already been fulfilled and scores of others to be fulfilled at Christ's return and during His eternal reign. The approach taken in the pages that follow is straightforward: As much as possible, we allow Scripture to speak for itself on matters of prophecy. We let God's Word reveal His intent and plan for Jesus's first time on earth and the events related to His second coming. We have included commentary on many passages simply to provide context and to clarify terms and references that might be unfamiliar to modern readers. Prophecies have been organized and grouped according to themes for easy navigation through this material.

It is our prayer that this book will serve as an open door for God to speak to your heart and mind regarding the Savior's life, ministry, and future reign. Most of all, may you draw courage and comfort in knowing that the Messiah we trust in and worship provides us absolute confidence because of the prophecies He has already fulfilled and the ones He will fulfill in the days to come.

UNDERSTANDING PROPHECY IN CONTEXT

In the history of the church, the prophetic portions of Scripture have suffered more from inadequate interpretation than any other major theological subject. The reason is that the church turned aside from a normal and literal interpretation of prophecy to one that is nonliteral and subject to the whims of the interpreter. This false approach to interpreting prophecy is contradicted by the fact that many hundreds of prophecies have already been literally fulfilled.

In the first two centuries of the Christian era, the church was predominantly "premillennial," interpreting Scripture to teach that Christ would fulfill the prophecy of His second coming to bring a thousand-year reign on earth before the eternal state began. This was considered normal in orthodox theology. The early interpretation of prophecy was not always cogent and was sometimes fanciful, but for the most part, prophecy was treated the same way as other scripture.

At the end of the second century and through the third century, the heretical school of theology at Alexandria, Egypt, advanced the errone-ous principle that the Bible should be interpreted in a nonliteral or allegorical sense. In applying this principle to the Scriptures, the school subverted all the major doctrines of the faith, including prophecy. The early church emphatically denied the Alexandrian system and to a large extent restored the interpretation of Scripture to its literal, grammatical, historical sense. The problem was that in prophecy there were predictions that had not yet been fulfilled. This made it more difficult to prove that literal fulfillment was true of prophecy. The result was somewhat catastrophic for the idea of a literal interpretation of prophecy, and the church floundered in the area of interpreting future events.

Augustine (AD 354–430) rescued the church from uncertainty as far as nonprophetic Scripture was concerned, but he continued to treat prophecy in a nonliteral way with the purpose of eliminating a millennial kingdom on earth. Strangely, Augustine held to a literal second coming, a literal heaven, and a literal hell, but not to a literal millennium. This arbitrary distinction has never been explained.

Because "amillennialism" (which denies a literal millennial kingdom on earth following the second coming) is essentially negative and hinders literal interpretation of prophecy, there was little progress in this area. The church continued to believe in heaven and hell and purgatory but neglected or dismissed Old Testament passages dealing with Israel in prophecy and the kingdom on earth. Even in the Protestant Reformation, prophecy was not rescued from this hindrance in its interpretation.

Though remnants of the church still advanced the premillennial view, it was not until the nineteenth and twentieth centuries that a serious movement began to restore the literal truth of prophecy. The twentieth century was especially significant in the progress of prophetic interpretation in that many details of prophecy were debated and clarified in a way not previously done.

The importance of prophecy should be evident, even superficially, in examining the Christian faith, since about one-fourth of the Bible was written as prophecy. It is evident that God intended to draw aside the veil of the future and to give some indication of what His plans and purposes were for the human race and for the universe as a whole. The neglect and misinterpretation of Scriptures supporting the premillennial interpretation are now to some extent being corrected.

For Christians, a solid hope for the future is essential. Christianity without a future would not be basic Christianity. In contrast to the beliefs of some other religions, which often paint the future in a forbidding way, Christianity's hope is bright and clear, assuring the Christian that the life to come will be better than the present one. As Paul stated in 2 Corinthians 5:8, "We are confident, I say, and would prefer to be away from the body and at home with the Lord." In the Christian faith, the future is painted as one of bliss and happiness in the presence of the Lord without the ills that are common to this life.

The revelation of prophecy in the Bible serves as important evidence that the Scriptures are accurate in their interpretation of the future. Because approximately half of the prophecies of the Bible have already been fulfilled in a literal way, we have a strong intellectual basis for assuming that prophecy yet to be fulfilled will likewise have a literal fulfillment. At the same time, we can rightly conclude that the Bible is inspired of the Holy Spirit and that prophecy is indeed a revelation by God for that which is certain to come.

Scriptural prophecy, properly interpreted, also provides a guideline for establishing the value of human conduct and the things that pertain to this life. For Christians, the ultimate question is whether

God considers what we are doing of value, in contrast to the world's system of values, which is largely materialistic.

Prophecy also provides a guide to the meaning of history. Though philosophers will continue to debate a philosophy of history, the Bible indicates that history is the unfolding of God's plan and purpose for revealing Himself and manifesting His love. In the Christian faith, history reaches its climax in God's plan for the future in which the earth in its present situation will be destroyed and a new earth will be created. A proper interpretation of prophecy serves to support and enhance all other areas of theology, and without a proper interpretation of prophecy, all other areas to some extent become incomplete revelation.

In attempting to accurately communicate the meaning of Scripture, prophecy serves to bring light and understanding to many aspects of our present life as well as our future hope. In an effort to understand and interpret prophecy correctly as a justifiable theological exercise, it is necessary to establish a proper base for interpretation.

1

WHO IS THE MESSIAH?

Each book of Scripture—from Genesis to Revelation, in the Old Testament and New Testament—can be thought of like a part of a map that points to one man: the Messiah. What does God's Word say about the signs of the Messiah? What are the characteristics of the Son of Man? Which events, miracles, and activities would have to take place in order to confirm Jesus as the chosen one?

As we journey through God's Word, a complete portrait of the Messiah will take shape. We hope that you take time to study and absorb these selected prophecies, all of which were confirmed in the person of Jesus Christ. Allow them to edify your faith and draw you closer to Him.

JUDGMENT AND PROMISE OF SALVATION

> And I will put enmity
> between you and the woman,
> and between your offspring and hers;
> he will crush your head,
> and you will strike his heel. (Gen. 3:15)

Genesis 3:14–24 is short, but its impact has sent ripples through every culture, community, family, and individual for the whole of human history. It was fulfilled by the spiritual death of Adam and Eve and their ultimate physical death (vv. 7–24). In fulfilling the prophecy of death, God added other prophecies, including the curse on the serpent (vv. 14–15). God prophesied that Eve would experience pain in childbirth. To Adam, God predicted that the ground would be cursed and Adam would have difficulty raising the food necessary for his continued existence. In the midst of these promises, which enlarged the judgment that had come on mankind because of the entrance of sin, a plan for redemption was also revealed.

In pronouncing the curse on the devil and the serpent, it was prophesied that there would always be enmity between the serpent and the descendants of the woman (v. 15). Referring to one of the woman's descendants (Christ), God said, "He will crush your head." In regard to the judgment on Satan, ensured by the cross of Christ, the prophecy was further enlarged: "You will strike his heel" (v. 15). This referred to the fact that Christ would die, but unlike the effect on Satan, Christ's death would be conquered by resurrection. This was fulfilled in Christ's death and resurrection (Rom. 3:24–25).

PROVISIONS OF THE COVENANT

> I will make you into a great nation,
>> and I will bless you;
> I will make your name great,
>> and you will be a blessing.
> I will bless those who bless you,

and whoever curses you I will curse;

and all peoples on earth

will be blessed through you. (Gen. 12:2–3)

God, in His goodness, cares for all the needs of His children. There is no need too small to capture His attention. In Genesis 12:1–3, God reveals His caring nature in the story of Abram, who was still in Ur of the Chaldeans.

The covenant with Abram was a major step in divine revelation, indicating that God had set Abram apart. Through Abram's line, God would bring salvation to mankind. Though only eleven chapters were used to trace the whole history of the world prior to Abram, including creation and all the major events that followed, the rest of the book of Genesis was devoted to Abram and his immediate descendants, indicating the importance of this covenant.

The covenant required Abram to leave his country and his people and go to the land that God would show him. The expression "you will be a blessing" (v. 2) could be translated "be a blessing." Abram was essential to God's program of bringing blessing and revelation to the world and ultimately salvation through Jesus Christ. In keeping with Abram's obedience, God made the promises: (1) "I will make you into a great nation"; (2) "I will bless you"; and (3) "I will make your name great" (v. 2).

PROMISE OF A FUTURE FAITHFUL PRIEST

I will raise up for myself a faithful priest, who will

do according to what is in my heart and mind. I will

> firmly establish his priestly house, and they will min-
> ister before my anointed one always. (1 Sam. 2:35)

In 1 Samuel 2:35–36, God made a declaration in contrast to the unfaithfulness of Hophni and Phinehas, reminding His people that He was the one who established and removed priests and rulers. The priesthood was taken away from Abiathar, who had descended from Eli, and instead was given to Zadok, who was a descendant of Eleazar, a son of Aaron (1 Kings 2:27, 35). This prophecy, however, seems to go beyond the immediate line of priests and was partially fulfilled by Samuel. It ultimately will be fulfilled by Jesus Christ, who is a priest forever (Ps. 110; Heb. 5:6; Rev. 19:16).

THE FAVOR OF DAVID PASSED DOWN THE GENERATIONS

> I will maintain my love to him forever,
>   and my covenant with him will never fail.
> I will establish his line forever,
>   his throne as long as the heavens endure.
>   (Ps. 89:28–29)

Psalm 89:19–37 is a testament to how incredible David's story is. When we first meet David, he is a humble shepherd boy, the youngest in a family of older, stronger men. Of all the men God could have selected to lead His people, David was the unlikeliest. Yet David rose to power and was declared "the most exalted of the kings of the earth" (v. 27). And God asserted that David's line would live on forever (vv. 28–29).

The people of Israel, however, were warned that if they sinned, God would punish them: "If his sons forsake my law and do not follow my statutes, if they violate my decrees and fail to keep my commands, I will punish their sin with the rod, their iniquity with flogging" (vv. 30–32). In spite of the possibility of Israel's sin, God promised that this would not alter the covenant:

> But I will not take my love from him,
>   nor will I ever betray my faithfulness.
> I will not violate my covenant
>   or alter what my lips have uttered.
> Once for all, I have sworn by my holiness—
>   and I will not lie to David—
> that his line will continue forever
>   and his throne endure before me like the sun;
> it will be established forever like the moon,
>   the faithful witness in the sky. (vv. 33–37)

Confirmation of this Davidic covenant is found in the words of the angel to Mary, announcing that she would be the mother of Jesus:

> Do not be afraid, Mary, for you have found favor with God. And behold, you will conceive in your womb and bring forth a Son, and shall call His name JESUS. He will be great, and will be called the Son of the Highest; and the Lord God will give Him the throne of His father David.

And He will reign over the house of Jacob forever, and of His kingdom there will be no end.
(Luke 1:30–33 NKJV)

In addition to the general promise that Jesus would be Mary's
son, the specific promises were given that He would occupy the
throne of His father David and that His reign and His kingdom
would never end.

MESSIANIC PROPHECY AND THE KINGDOM

Ask me,
> and I will make the nations your inheritance,
> the ends of the earth your possession.
You will break them with a rod of iron;
> you will dash them to pieces like pottery.
> (Ps. 2:8–9)

Psalm 2 describes God's purpose to establish His Son as King
on Mount Zion. The opening verses prophesy the rebellion of the
world against the Lord. In response, "the One enthroned in heaven
laughs; the Lord scoffs at them" (v. 4). This describes the attitude of
God toward worldly power. In God's prophetic purpose, however,
He rebuked them in anger and terrified them in wrath, saying, "I
have installed my King on Zion, my holy mountain" (v. 6). The Lord
also declared His eternal decree (vv. 7–9), and God the Father was
revealed as saying to the Son, "You are my son; today I have become
your father" (v. 7). This will be fulfilled in the millennium.

Biblical scholars have interpreted this passage in various ways because it refers to the sonship of Christ. The best interpretation is that Jesus Christ has always been a Son in relation to the Father but that the declaration of this was made in time. Some scholars have advanced other views, such as that Christ became the Son by incarnation, by baptism, or by resurrection. The interpretation also relates to the question as to whether Christ was a Son eternally by eternal generation. In John 3:16, God is declared to have given "His only begotten Son" (NKJV). Because the word *begotten* implies beginning in time, it seems a contradiction of eternal sonship.

Probably the best solution is to hold that it refers to Christ's eternal sonship—with the thought of having the life of the Father—without complicating it with the concept of a beginning. Isaiah 9:6 refers to Christ as "a son" who "is given." Because the decree of God that declared Christ a Son is eternal, evidence seems to support the concept that He is eternally His Son but that the revelation of this truth is made in time.

Important to this purpose of God is the fact that He will subdue all things under the Son: "I will make the nations your inheritance, the ends of the earth your possession. You will break them with a rod of iron; you will dash them to pieces like pottery" (Ps. 2:8–9). The fact that Christ will rule as an absolute monarch is supported by other prophecies. Revelation 19:15 declares, "Coming out of his mouth is a sharp sword with which to strike down the nations. 'He will rule them with an iron scepter.'" In interpreting this passage, it is quite clear that Christ did not accomplish this at His first coming and that the premillennial interpretation that He will accomplish this after His second coming fits the prophetic scriptures on this subject. The messianic psalms generally picture Christ on the throne of the Father now awaiting His future triumph, when He will subdue the earth and sit on the throne of David.

In view of this coming judgment, kings and rulers were exhorted to "serve the LORD with fear, and rejoice with trembling. Kiss the Son, lest He be angry, and you perish in the way, when His wrath is kindled but a little. Blessed are all those who put their trust in Him" (Ps. 2:11–12 NKJV).

Early in the book of Psalms, this general theme of the coming King is made a central revelation. In the Davidic covenant, David was declared to be a son of God (2 Sam. 7:14). How much more is the eternal Son of God the rightful King who will reign on the throne of David.

TAKING DAVID'S PATH

> Therefore my heart is glad and my tongue rejoices;
>   my body also will rest secure,
> because you will not abandon me to the realm of
>   the dead,
>   nor will you let your faithful one see decay.
>   (Ps. 16:9–10)

Psalm 16 is considered one of the messianic psalms because Peter quoted verses 8–11 (Acts 2:25–28) and Paul quoted verse 10 at Antioch (Acts 13:35). David expressed his faith that he would not be abandoned to the grave (Ps. 16:10), referring to himself, but he added that God would not "let your faithful one see decay" (v. 10).

This was fulfilled by Christ, as David's body did decay. David would continue in the grave, but in his resurrection he would experience "the path of life" (v. 11).

As used by Peter and Paul, Psalm 16:10 refers to Christ's resurrection and was quoted as proof that the resurrection of Christ was predicted. Others today can enjoy fellowship with God as long as they live and have the assurance that when they die, though their bodies may be placed in the grave, they are subject to future resurrection and meanwhile will enjoy fellowship with God in heaven.

PURSUED BY THE LORD'S GOODNESS

> The LORD is my shepherd, I lack nothing.
> (Ps. 23:1)

Psalm 23 is not usually included among the messianic psalms, but the role of the Lord as David's shepherd anticipated the role of Christ as the Good Shepherd, who would care for His flock in this present life.

David declared that he lacked nothing (v. 1), that his soul would be restored (v. 3), and that he would "walk through the valley of the shadow of death" without fearing evil (v. 4 NKJV). The Lord's goodness followed him all the days of his life, and he had the hope of dwelling in the house of the Lord forever (vv. 5–6). Psalm 23 parallels the experience of present-age believers, who are nourished and restored spiritually, are led by the Lord in their walk, and are protected by Him in times of danger.

THE COMING SON OF DAVID

> For to us a child is born,
>   to us a son is given,
>   and the government will be on his
>   shoulders.
> And he will be called
>   Wonderful Counselor, Mighty God,
>   Everlasting Father, Prince of Peace.
> Of the greatness of his government and peace
>   there will be no end. (Isa. 9:6–7)

In the short sentences of Isaiah 9:1–7, the hope of the world is restored. This prophecy describes the coming of the Savior and portrays Jesus's birth as a time when a great light would shine (v. 2), declaring it a time of joy and rejoicing (v. 3). This event was depicted as a great victory for Israel (vv. 4–5).

As we saw in Psalm 89, God promised David that his kingdom would go on forever, being fulfilled by the millennial kingdom. God will continue to be sovereign over creation throughout eternity to come.

The prophecy specified that His throne would be David's throne (Isa. 9:7), in fulfillment of the Davidic covenant indicating that this throne, like David's kingdom, would be on earth, not in heaven.

This kingdom will be distinguished as one of justice and righteousness (cf. 11:3–5) and will be realized through the power of God: "The zeal of the LORD Almighty will accomplish this" (9:7).

THE CROWNING OF JOSHUA

> Here is the man whose name is the Branch, and he
> will branch out from his place and build the temple
> of the LORD. It is he who will build the temple of
> the LORD, and he will be clothed with majesty and
> will sit and rule on his throne. And he will be a
> priest on his throne. And there will be harmony
> between the two. (Zech. 6:12–13)

In the revelation in Zechariah 6:9–15, the Lord instructed Zechariah to take silver and gold from three exiles—Heldai, Tobijah, and Jedaiah—and with the silver and gold make a crown to be set on the head of the high priest Joshua, the son of Jozadak (vv. 9–11).

The fact that Joshua the high priest was crowned rather than Zerubbabel, the governor, indicated that God was guarding against the idea that Zerubbabel was the fulfillment of God's promise for the descendant of David to sit on a throne.

In the crowning, Joshua was taken as Israel's representative of the coming Messiah; and in verses 12–13, the prophecy regarding the branch and the building of the temple was given.

As Joshua had a relatively minor role in the rebuilding of the temple, the fulfillment must go on to the Messiah, Jesus Christ, in His second coming when He will fulfill the prophecy completely and be both king (Isa. 9:7; Jer. 23:5; Mic. 4:3, 7; Zeph. 3:15; Zech. 14:9) and priest (Heb. 4:15; 5:6; 7:11–21). A priest of the Levitical order could not sit on a throne and reign, but Christ will be both king and priest and will combine the two offices in His person and work.

2

THE ONCE AND FUTURE KING

The mysteries of Scripture are seemingly endless, and contemplating them can be daunting. We know that Jesus was the ruler and savior of all creation, even before the foundations of the world were laid. But how can it be that Jesus's lordship was, is, and is yet to come? The following passages shed light on the beautiful complexities of Jesus, our once and future king.

PSALMS OF THE COMING KING OF GLORY

> Lift up your heads, you gates;
>> lift them up, you ancient doors,
>> that the King of glory may come in.
> Who is he, this King of glory?
>> The LORD Almighty—
>> he is the King of glory. (Ps. 24:9–10)

Psalm 24 is not usually considered a messianic psalm, and yet its wording goes far beyond anything that David experienced. Some believe it was written in connection with the ark being brought into

Jerusalem and placed in the temple (2 Sam. 6). The importance of "clean hands and a pure heart" was essential to receiving the blessing from God (Ps. 24:4–5). The references to the "King of glory" (vv. 7–10) obviously went beyond the experience of David as king of Israel and anticipated the Lord's coming to claim the earth in His second coming.

> Your throne, O God, will last for ever and ever;
> a scepter of justice will be the scepter of your
> kingdom. (Ps. 45:6)

Psalm 45 is classified as a messianic psalm because verse 6 refers to David's throne as eternal (2 Sam. 7:16), and this verse is quoted in Hebrews 1:8 regarding the ultimate rule of Christ on earth. As Scripture states, God's "throne … will last for ever and ever" (Ps. 45:6), and His rule will be characterized by righteousness and justice.

Psalm 45:8–9 pictures the king on his wedding day. The beauty of the bride is described in verse 11: "Let the king be enthralled by your beauty; honor him, for he is your lord." Her garments are "interwoven with gold" (v. 13) and beautifully "embroidered" (v. 14). Future children of the bride are called princes, and their memory will be perpetuated (vv. 16–17).

Though the psalm seems to refer to a wedding of David, it is remarkably similar to the concept of Christ and His bride. The apostle John may have had this passage in mind in Revelation 19:6–10. The psalm as a whole, therefore, is typical of Christ as the king and son of David and will be fulfilled in the rapture.

Be still, and know that I am God;
> I will be exalted among the nations,
> I will be exalted in the earth. (Ps. 46:10)

Psalm 46:4–10 tells of God making wars cease and being exalted among the nations (vv. 9–10). This will not be fulfilled literally until Christ returns in His second coming.

When you ascended on high,
> you took many captives;
> you received gifts from people. (Ps. 68:18)

Psalm 68:18–21 says Christ will lead captives in His ascension (see also Eph. 4:8) and crush the heads of His enemies. This was fulfilled in David's lifetime and will be fulfilled by Christ at His second coming (Rev. 19:11–15).

May all kings bow down to him
> and all nations serve him.
For he will deliver the needy who cry out,
> the afflicted who have no one to help.
> (Ps. 72:11–12)

Psalm 72, generally speaking, predicts that the righteous will prosper and the wicked will be judged. According to the inscription, it was written by Solomon and is one of two psalms he wrote (see also Ps. 127). Psalm 72 begins with a prayer for the king and then prophesies his successful reign (vv. 1–3).

As the psalm unfolds, however, it goes far beyond anything that Solomon himself could fulfill. In verse 5, the king is predicted to "endure as long as the sun, as long as the moon, through all generations." Likewise in verse 7, Solomon stated, "In his days may the righteous flourish and prosperity abound till the moon is no more." These prophecies obviously look beyond the reign of Solomon and anticipate the reign of Christ in the millennium and ultimately His eternal reign (Isa. 2:1–5).

The fact that all kings will be under him, as stated in Psalm 72:11, was relatively fulfilled by Solomon because the kings in his area bowed to him; but obviously, this did not include the whole globe. Of both Christ and Solomon it could be said, "May his name endure forever; may it continue as long as the sun" (v. 17). Though Solomon would not live forever, his good name has been perpetuated by the scriptures that describe his reign. The final prayer anticipates that "the whole earth" will "be filled with his glory" (v. 19), to be fulfilled in the millennium.

And the closing of the psalm states, "This concludes the prayers of David son of Jesse" (v. 20). However, according to the inscriptions, David was the author of other psalms, such as Psalms 86, 101, 103, and many others. Psalm 72 supports the premillennial interpretation of Scripture, as it does not find fulfillment in history. The scene is earth, not heaven, and its identification of the Euphrates River (v. 8) makes clear that it will not be the new earth of Revelation 21–22.

I have made a covenant with my chosen one,
I have sworn to David my servant,

"I will establish your line forever
and make your throne firm through all
generations." (Ps. 89:3–4)

Psalm 89:1–37 shows God, in a touching display of loyalty and generosity, declaring a promise to David and confirming the covenant revealed in 2 Samuel 7:11–16. The psalm also proclaims that God's love for David will continue forever, that his covenant will never fail, and that his throne will endure as long as the heavens do (Ps. 89:28–37; Jer. 23:5–8). The contingency of disobedience on the part of his descendants was faced. God promised that if they forsook His covenant and His commands, He would punish them but He would not reverse the covenant: "But I will not take my love from him, nor will I ever betray my faithfulness. I will not violate my covenant or alter what my lips have uttered. Once for all, I have sworn by my holiness—and I will not lie to David—that his line will continue forever and his throne endure before me like the sun; it will be established forever like the moon, the faithful witness in the sky" (Ps. 89:33–37).

Any interpretation that takes these words in their normal meanings, relating these promises to the Davidic covenant and to the kingdom on earth, will find that the only possible complete fulfillment is through Christ Himself following His second coming.

Let all creation rejoice before the LORD, for he
comes,
he comes to judge the earth.
He will judge the world in righteousness
and the peoples in his faithfulness. (Ps. 96:13)

Psalm 96 shows the anticipation for the time when the Lord will reign over the earth and judge people with justice. It is described as a time of joy on earth.

> Let the rivers clap their hands,
>> let the mountains sing together for joy;
> let them sing before the LORD,
>> for he comes to judge the earth. (Ps. 98:8–9)

Psalm 98 speaks of the joy on earth when the Lord reigns. The whole of creation will rejoice under the reign of the Creator and Father.

> The LORD says to my lord:

> "Sit at my right hand
>> until I make your enemies
>> a footstool for your feet." (Ps. 110:1)

Psalm 110 is classified as a messianic psalm because it clearly refers to Jesus Christ as king. Christ is also declared "a priest forever, in the order of Melchizedek" (v. 4). His judgment in the millennial kingdom is mentioned: "The Lord is at your right hand; he will crush kings on the day of his wrath. He will judge the nations, heaping up the dead and crushing the rulers of the whole earth" (vv. 5–6). This obviously is a reference to the beginning of the millennial kingdom after the second coming of Christ. This is fulfilled in history and prophecy.

> The LORD swore an oath to David,
>> a sure oath he will not revoke:
> "One of your own descendants
>> I will place on your throne.
> If your sons keep my covenant
>> and the statutes I teach them,
> then their sons will sit
>> on your throne for ever and ever."
>> (Ps. 132:11–12)

Psalm 132:11–18 reports the oath that God made to David (vv. 11–12) and then states, "For the LORD has chosen Zion, he has desired it for his dwelling … I will bless her with abundant provisions; her poor I will satisfy with food" (vv. 13, 15). This is fulfilled in history and prophecy.

THE FUTURE MESSIANIC KINGDOM

> The mountain of the LORD's temple will be
>> established
> as the highest of the mountains. (Isa. 2:2)

In Isaiah 2:1–11, the prophet predicted the future kingdom of the Messiah. He wrote, "In the last days the mountain of the LORD's temple … will be exalted above the hills, and all nations will stream to it" (v. 2; see also Zech. 14:16). Jerusalem is described as the capital of the world in a time of peace rather than war, a time when the Lord will teach His ways (Isa. 2:3–5). This will be fulfilled in the millennium.

THE FUTURE GLORIOUS KINGDOM OF ISRAEL

A shoot will come up from the stump of Jesse;
 from his roots a Branch will bear fruit.
The Spirit of the LORD will rest on him.
   (Isa. 11:1–2)

In Isaiah 11–12, the prophet predicted that Israel would enjoy the future glorious kingdom. Having cut down Assyria as a tree is cut down (10:33–34), now God would raise up a new "shoot," which "will come up from the stump of Jesse" (11:1). This branch that comes from the root of Jesse, or David's line, "will bear fruit" (v. 1). This was fulfilled by the birth of Jesus Christ in His first coming.

The passage, however, reveals primarily Christ's position as king and judge at the time of His second coming. It was prophesied that the Holy Spirit would rest on Him and that He would have wisdom, power, and knowledge (v. 2). His judgment will be with justice (vv. 3–4). He "will slay the wicked" (v. 4), and "righteousness" and "faithfulness" will characterize His rule (v. 5). These prophecies, of course, will be fulfilled at the time of the second coming of Christ and do not refer to God's present rule on earth.

The future kingdom reign of Christ will be characterized by peace among animals as well as among people. Wolf and lamb will live together, and "the leopard will lie down with the goat, the calf and the lion and the yearling together" (v. 6). The peacefulness of nature is summarized in verse 9: "They will neither harm nor destroy on all my holy mountain, for the earth will be filled with

the knowledge of the LORD as the waters cover ᴜ.
be obvious that any literal fulfillment of this passage
millennial kingdom after the second coming of Christ. Even ᴜ.
nonliteral sense, this does not describe the present age. To apply it
to heaven or to the new heaven and the new earth, as some amillenarians hold, again does not fit the picture provided in other
scriptures of heaven and of the new earth.

The restoration of Israel in the time of Christ's reign on earth will
follow His second coming (vv. 10–16). The "Root of Jesse," referring
to Christ, will be the One to whom the nations rally (v. 10). Israel
will be regathered from the nations to which she was scattered (vv.
11–12). The animosity between the kingdom of Judah and the kingdom of Israel will vanish, and Ephraim and Judah will be at peace.
Together they will bring into subjection their former enemies (vv.
13–14). To assist the regathering of Israel, "the gulf of the Egyptian
sea" may "dry up" and the Euphrates River will not be a formidable
water barrier (v. 15). While this may be supernatural, Russia has
already helped build a dam across the Euphrates River, and when this
and other dams are closed, the Euphrates River dries up in several
sections. The drying up of the Euphrates River will permit people to
cross easily (see Rev. 16:12).

Because of their great victory, Israel will praise the Lord (Isa. 12).
The glorious restoration of Israel and their joy in the future kingdom
was anticipated in the Abrahamic covenant (Gen. 12:1–3; 15:18–21;
17:7–8; 22:17–18), the Davidic covenant (2 Sam. 7:16), and the
new covenant (Jer. 31:33–34). The glorious future millennial kingdom of Israel will be in contrast to the predicted fall of Babylon and
Assyria (Isa. 10:5–19; 13:1–22).

THE COMING OF CHRIST, THE RIGHTEOUS KING

> See, a king will reign in righteousness,
> and rulers will rule with justice. (Isa. 32:1)

In Isaiah 32, the prophet predicted that Israel at that time would listen to God's exhortation (vv. 2–8). Israel was promised severe judgment from God but ultimate restoration and deliverance (vv. 9–20). The passage concludes, "How blessed you will be, sowing your seed by every stream, and letting your cattle and donkeys range free" (v. 20).

THE MILLENNIAL KINGDOM ESTABLISHED

> The LORD will be king over the whole earth. On
> that day there will be one LORD, and his name the
> only name. (Zech. 14:9)

Zechariah 14:9–21 reveals the millennial kingdom will be distinguished by the fact that the Lord, Jesus Christ as the Messiah of Israel and King of Kings, will rule over the entire earth. Included in the topographical changes will be the elevation of Jerusalem as described in verse 10. From that day forward, Jerusalem will be secure and will never be destroyed again.

An indication of the rule of Christ as King of Kings and Lord of Lords is that He will judge the nations that fought against Jerusalem (vv. 12–13). A plague will seize humans and beast alike, but in the

results, a great quantity of gold, silver, and clothing will accrue to
Israel's benefit (v. 14).

Those who survive the purging judgments at the beginning of
the millennial kingdom will be required to worship Christ annually
(v. 16). If they do not worship Him as commanded, God will hold
their rain (vv. 17–19). It will be a time when the holiness of God is
especially revealed, and false elements like the Canaanites will be shut
out (vv. 20–21). The partial revelation of the nature of the millennial
kingdom as described here is amplified in many other scriptures in
both the Old Testament and the New Testament.

3

THE MARKERS OF THE MESSIAH: PROPHECIES OF JESUS'S BIRTH AND MINISTRY

Over the years, Israel saw the rise and fall of many kings. The eyes of God's people were looking for the promised one, but how would they tell this special king apart from all the ordinary kings? This one would be different from any other, as we clearly see in the following passages.

PARABLES AND THE PAST

> I will open my mouth with a parable;
> > I will utter hidden things, things from of old.
> > (Ps. 78:2)

Psalm 78:1–4 says the coming Messiah will speak in parables and will reveal things formerly hidden. Jesus was known for telling stories and parables in order to illustrate a point. Moreover, He referenced the teachings that had been passed down through the generations, demonstrating an intimate familiarity and mastery of the Law.

THE SIGN OF IMMANUEL'S BIRTH

> Therefore the Lord Himself will give you a sign:
> The virgin will conceive and give birth to a son, and
> will call him Immanuel. (Isa. 7:14)

According to Isaiah 7, the attack on Judah by Ephraim will not be successful (vv. 1–9). This was fulfilled in the events that followed. Isaiah recorded that "the LORD spoke to Ahaz, 'Ask the LORD your God for a sign, whether in the deepest depths or in the highest heights'" (v. 10). God promised that a sign would be given to Israel: "The virgin will conceive and give birth to a son, and will call him Immanuel. He will be eating curds and honey when he knows enough to reject the wrong and choose the right, for before the boy knows enough to reject the wrong and choose the right, the land of the two kings you dread will be laid waste. The LORD will bring on you and on your people and on the house of your father a time unlike any since Ephraim broke away from Judah—he will bring the king of Assyria" (vv. 14–17). Isaiah predicted the invasion of the king of Assyria and the destruction of the land (vv. 18–25).

The prophecy concerning a virgin with child has been variously considered by scholars. Some believe it referred to a contemporary situation in which a young woman, still a virgin and about to be married, would bear a child, fulfilling the prophecy. Another point of view is that the prophecy is exclusively messianic and refers to the fact that Mary, while still a virgin, would be the mother of Christ (Matt. 1:18, 25), which according to Matthew 1:21–23, was a fulfillment of the prophecy of Isaiah. Still others consider this prophecy as referring to both, that is, a contemporary reference to a child whose birth was mentioned in Isaiah 8 and whose ultimate prophetic fulfillment was the birth of Christ.

THE COMING RESTORATION OF ISRAEL

> In the wilderness prepare
> the way for the LORD;
> make straight in the desert
> a highway for our God. (Isa. 40:3)

Isaiah 40 is the beginning of the final major section of the book of Isaiah. There is ample evidence that Isaiah wrote this as well as the first thirty-nine chapters, but the prophetic emphasis shifts. In keeping with the purpose of God's revelation, a major change in theme of this section was God's plan for restoration and deliverance of His people. This will primarily be fulfilled after the second coming of Christ in the millennial kingdom. At that time, not only will Israel receive blessings she does not deserve, but also judgment will fall on Babylon because of her sins. In view of Israel's glorious future, she is exhorted to live righteously before the Lord.

The prophet began with a message of comfort for the people of God. He assured them that their time of trial was about over and that they would receive from "the LORD's hand double for all [their] sins" (v. 2), which indicated forgiveness. Prophecy was revealed concerning the voice of one preceding the Messiah: "A voice of one calling: 'In the wilderness prepare the way for the LORD; make straight in the desert a highway for our God. Every valley shall be raised up, every mountain and hill made low; the rough ground shall become level, the rugged places a plain. And the glory of the LORD will be revealed, and all people will see it together. For the mouth of the LORD has spoken'" (vv. 3–5).

All four gospels attribute this passage to John the Baptist as the forerunner of Christ (Matt. 3:1–4; Mark 1:2–4; Luke 1:76–79; John 1:23). In this passage, the entire nation of Israel is pictured as in a desert place (Isa. 40:3) and awaiting the glorious deliverance of God. Leveling the ground was a way of preparing for the coming of a king, and the passage anticipates the millennial kingdom: "And the glory of the LORD will be revealed" (v. 5).

GOD'S BELOVED SERVANT

> Here is my servant, whom I uphold,
>   my chosen one in whom I delight;
> I will put my Spirit on him
>   and he will bring justice to the nations.
>   (Isa. 42:1)

Isaiah 42:1–13 presents the revelation concerning the servant of the Lord. Isaiah 42:1 is the first presentation of Christ as "the servant" in contrast to Israel as the servant of God. The "servant" in this section is none other than Christ Himself, though some regard it as a reference to Israel. This is the first of four songs presenting the servant as Christ (42:1–9; 49:1–13; 50:4–11; 52:13–53:12).

Isaiah 42:2–4 continues to describe Christ: "He will not shout or cry out, or raise his voice in the streets. A bruised reed he will not

break, and a smoldering wick he will not snuff out. In faithfulness
he will bring forth justice; he will not falter or be discouraged till he
establishes justice on earth. In his teaching the islands will put their
hope" (see also the partial quotation of vv. 1–4 in Matt. 12:18–21).

Israel was a blind servant in contrast to Christ, who will bring
justice and restoration to the world (Isa. 42:19). God as the Creator
would be the One who gives life to His people (v. 5). God promised
to take Israel by the hand, regard them as a covenant people, and
make them "a light for the Gentiles" (v. 6). The fact that Christ will
be a light to the Gentiles (v. 16) is mentioned in Luke 1:79. God
will not only deliver the people as a whole but also open individual
eyes that were blind and free captives of sin. In keeping with this,
in Isaiah a voice of praise to the Lord is recorded and the Lord's
ultimate victory is described (Isa. 42:10–13). This was fulfilled in
Christ's first coming and will be fulfilled in His second coming.

SALVATION FOR THE GENTILES

> My house will be called
> a house of prayer for all nations. (Isa. 56:7)

In Isaiah 56:1–8, God promised to include among the blessed
those who were not Jews but who kept the Sabbaths and who loved
and served the Lord. Their offerings would be accepted, and they
would have joy in the house of prayer (v. 7). The statement that "my
house will be called a house of prayer" (v. 7) was quoted by Christ
as a rebuke of Israel's desecration of the temple (Matt. 21:13). This
is fulfilled in history and will be fulfilled in the millennium. Isaiah

56 closes with a severe indictment on the wicked in contrast to the blessings pronounced on those who serve the Lord.

THE PROMISED REDEEMER TO COME IN SPITE OF ISRAEL'S SINS

> The Redeemer will come to Zion,
>> to those in Jacob who repent of their sins.
>> (Isa. 59:20)

Isaiah 59 is a graphic description of Israel's sins that calls for confession and restoration. God declared how her sins had separated her from Him (vv. 1–4). Her acts of violence (v. 6) and injustice (vv. 8–14) demanded a divine answer to Israel as well as to her enemies (v. 18). The Redeemer will come out of Zion to those who repent of their sins (v. 20), and God promised that His Spirit would speak through them forever (v. 21). This was fulfilled in the first coming and will be fulfilled in the second coming.

THE NEW COVENANT

> I will put my law in their minds
>> and write it on their hearts.
> I will be their God,
>> and they will be my people. (Jer. 31:33)

In Jeremiah 31:31–40, God declared He would make a new covenant with Israel. This would be in contrast to the Mosaic covenant He gave them in Egypt (v. 32). The continuation of this passage affirms a drastically different dynamic between creation and Creator: "'No longer will they teach their neighbor, or say to one another, "Know the LORD," because they will all know me, from the least of them to the greatest,' declares the LORD. 'For I will forgive their wickedness and will remember their sins no more'" (v. 34).

This is one of the great prophecies in the Old Testament that describes the new covenant God will make, a gracious covenant stemming from the death of Christ, making it possible for God to forgive Israel as well as the Gentiles who come to Him. Though God in grace has saved and blessed Israel in the past, the major fulfillment for Israel will be after the second coming when she will be regathered to her land.

The absolute certainty of the new covenant is described in Jeremiah 31:35–36. The new covenant would be as sure as the natural laws that move the moon and the stars and stir up the sea. As long as these laws of nature would continue, God would continue His promises to Israel. This covenant is not a conditional one as the Mosaic covenant was.

Just as Israel will be graciously forgiven under the new covenant, so also the church in the present age receives grace. All grace systems stem from the death of Christ, whether applied to Israel or to other peoples. Hence, the church in the present age also participates in a new covenant. This can best be explained as one new covenant of grace made possible by the death of Christ, whether applied to Israel as in Jeremiah or to the church as in the New Testament. All grace has its origin in the new promise of grace, which has various applications. Jeremiah makes its application to Israel, which will largely be fulfilled in connection with the coming kingdom on earth following the second coming.

The second reassuring pledge of the Lord declared that only if the heavens could be measured and the foundations of the earth be searched out would He reject the descendants of Israel (Jer. 31:37). As a matter of fact, even our modern society with our great telescopes has not been able to find the end of the universe. The continuation of the sun and moon is a constant reminder that God is still keeping His promises to Israel and preserving her as a nation. The new covenant is a major prophetic revelation given further treatment in the New Testament, and its gracious promises will continue forever.

In the time related to the future kingdom, God declared:

> This city [Jerusalem] will be rebuilt for me from the Tower of Hananel to the Corner Gate. The measuring line will stretch from there straight to the hill of Gareb and then turn to Goah. The whole valley where dead bodies and ashes are thrown, and all the terraces out to the Kidron Valley on the east as far as the corner of the Horse Gate, will be holy to the LORD. The city will never again be uprooted or demolished. (Jer. 31:38–40)

This remarkable prophecy, given by Jeremiah almost twenty-five hundred years ago, has seen modern fulfillment in the recapture of Jerusalem. Modern Jerusalem has built up this precise area, and today there are lovely apartments and streets in a location formerly used as a place for garbage heaps and dead bodies. In spite of the fact that Jerusalem has been destroyed many times, God declared that this section would not be demolished but would continue to be holy to the Lord until the second coming. This prophecy is one of the signs that the coming of the Lord may be near.

ISRAEL'S FAITHLESS SHEPHERDS CONTRASTED WITH HER FUTURE TRUE SHEPHERD

> I will place over them one shepherd, my servant David, and he will tend them; he will tend them and be their shepherd. I the LORD will be their God, and my servant David will be prince among them. (Ezek. 34:23–24)

In Ezekiel 34, we see the Israelites had been led astray because they had false shepherds who did not care for them but "ruled them harshly and brutally" (v. 4). No one had attempted to find the sheep who were scattered (v. 6), and God declared that He was going to hold the shepherds accountable for their failure to tend to the sheep of Israel (vv. 7–10). This was fulfilled in the Babylonian captivity. God then promised to rescue the sheep in Israel's future restoration (v. 10).

God declared that He Himself would search for His sheep and rescue them from where they had been scattered (vv. 11–12). He promised, "I will bring them out from the nations and gather them from the countries, and I will bring them into their own land. I will pasture them on the mountains of Israel, in the ravines and in all the settlements in the land" (v. 13). This prediction of the future regathering of

Israel from all over the world is still an unfulfilled commitment that will be fulfilled when the coming millennial kingdom begins.

God will especially care for those who are weak or injured, will bring them to rich pastures, and will shepherd them with justice (vv. 14–16). This will be fulfilled in the millennium (Jer. 23:5–8). God promised special care for those who were weak and who had been trampled by the stronger sheep. He will serve as judge "between the fat sheep and the lean sheep" (Ezek. 34:20).

Central to God's plan of restoration for Israel will be the resurrection of David as a true shepherd who will serve as a prince under Christ as King of Kings and Lord of Lords (vv. 23–24). This places the fulfillment at the second coming when Old Testament saints will be resurrected (Dan. 12:1–3). God also promised that this would be a time of peace when the wild beasts would not afflict them, when they would receive showers to water the land, and when trees would bear their fruit (Ezek. 34:25–27).

Moreover, God promised to keep them in safety, no longer allowing the nations to plunder them, and would deliver them from famine (vv. 28–29). As a result of God's work in the restoration of Israel, "they will know that I, the LORD their God, am with them and that they, the Israelites, are my people, declares the Sovereign LORD. You are my sheep, the sheep of my pasture, and I am your God, declares the Sovereign LORD" (vv. 30–31).

CHRIST'S VICTORY THROUGH ATONEMENT

> Seventy "sevens" are decreed for your people and
> your holy city to finish transgression, to put an end

to sin, to atone for wickedness, to bring in everlasting righteousness. (Dan. 9:24)

In the Daniel 9:24 prophecy, God promised He would take up various causes on behalf of His people. These achievements would be marks of God's glory and His plan for fallen Israel. All of the achievements can be seen as markers of the coming Messiah, but two in particular should be noted.

The first achievement, "to atone for wickedness," refers both to the death of Christ on the cross, which is the basis for all grace, and the application of this, especially to Israel, at the time of the second coming. The expression "to atone" literally means "to cover." The death of Christ deals with sin in the final way that the sacrifices of the Old Testament could only illustrate temporarily. When Christ died on the cross, He brought in permanent reconciliation for those who would turn to Him in faith (2 Cor. 5:19).

The second achievement, "to bring in everlasting righteousness," was made possible by the death of Christ on the cross. The application of this to Israel individually and nationally relates to the second coming. As stated in Jeremiah 23:5–6, "'The days are coming,' declares the LORD, 'when I will raise up for David a righteous Branch, a King who will reign wisely and do what is just and right in the land. In his days Judah will be saved and Israel will live in safety. This is the name by which he will be called: The LORD Our Righteous Savior.'"

The time of this is the second coming, the same time that David will be resurrected to be a regent under Christ (Jer. 30:9). Righteousness is one of the outstanding characteristics of the millennial kingdom in contrast to previous dispensations.

A FATHER'S RELENTLESS LOVE

> When Israel was a child, I loved him,
> and out of Egypt I called my son.
> (Hosea 11:1)

How touching are the verses in Hosea 11:1–4, which demonstrate the Father's tender affection for His children! In His unfailing love, God led the children of Israel out of Egypt and back into His holy presence. Some interpret this passage as not simply a recollection of God's mercies but as a prophecy that Christ would come out of Egypt (v. 1; Matt. 2:15).

THE BIRTHPLACE OF THE MESSIAH

> But you, Bethlehem Ephrathah,
> though you are small among the clans of
> Judah,
> out of you will come for me
> one who will be ruler over Israel,
> whose origins are from of old,
> from ancient times. (Micah 5:2)

As foretold in Micah 5:1–5, in contrast to predictions of judgment, the future ruler of Israel (Christ) would come to Bethlehem. This was and will be fulfilled in Christ. Until this future ruler takes over, "Israel will be abandoned" (v. 3). When the ruler comes, however, He will "stand and shepherd his flock in the strength of the LORD" (v. 4). He will cause Israel to dwell securely and live in peace (vv. 4–5).

OUR HOPE IS SECURE IN GOD

> I will send my messenger, who will prepare the way
> before me. (Mal. 3:1)

In Malachi 2:17–3:5, the people had made the charge, "'All who do evil are good in the eyes of the LORD, and he is pleased with them' or 'Where is the God of justice?'" (2:17). The problem of how the wicked may prosper temporarily, apparently without check from God, is a frequent subject of Scripture (Job 21:7–26; Ps. 73:1–14; Eccl. 8:14).

Scripture, however, makes plain that while the wicked may prosper for a time, ultimately justice from God will come on them (Job 24:22–24; Ps. 73:16–20; Eccl. 8:12–13). Scripture frequently refers to the fact that God will bring in His righteous kingdom as the climax to human history in the period following the second coming of Christ.

While the people still questioned whether God was just, God was going to send His messenger to prepare the way of the Lord (Mal. 3:1). This reference was to John the Baptist, according to the New Testament (Matt. 11:10; Mark 1:2; Luke 7:27), but the phrase "the Lord you are seeking" (Mal. 3:1) was not quoted in the New Testament. It was true that when Christ came, He came suddenly to His temple at His first coming. But the final second coming of Christ will be one of judgment, not of grace.

As is so often true in the Old Testament, both the first coming of Christ and the second coming of Christ are considered one event. None of the prophets seem to have understood the separation of these events by a long period between. The messenger obviously was John the Baptist, however, and Christ was the One who would come suddenly in His first coming and will come again suddenly in His second coming.

THE FINAL WORD

> See, I will send the prophet Elijah to you before
> that great and dreadful day of the LORD comes.
> (Mal. 4:5)

Malachi 4 marks the end of the Old Testament. By way of conclusion to the entire book as well as by way of spiritual preparation for the coming days, God declared, "Remember the law of my servant Moses, the decrees and laws I gave him at Horeb for all Israel" (v. 4). The law that God delivered through Moses was His word to the people of Israel, including the commands to follow righteousness and prohibit evil. They were given the promise that they would be blessed if they kept the law but cursed if they rejected it. History has demonstrated the truth about this prediction.

The final word from Malachi predicted the coming of Elijah: "See, I will send the prophet Elijah to you before that great and dreadful day of the LORD comes. He will turn the hearts of the parents to their children, and the hearts of the children to their parents; or else I will come and strike the land with total destruction" (vv. 5–6).

Interpreters have differed as to whether this prophecy of Elijah was fulfilled by John the Baptist. According to Matthew 11:7–10, the messenger of Malachi 3:1 was identified specifically to be John the Baptist and, as such, one who prepared the way of the Lord in His first coming. It was predicted before his birth that John would operate in the spirit and power of Elijah (Luke 1:17).

4

THE MISSION OF THE MESSIAH: PROPHECIES OF JESUS'S DEATH AND RESURRECTION

Christ did not come to earth to be merely a ruler, another triumphant king. He also was, is, and will be a servant—even unto death. The death of the Messiah is foretold just as consistently as His unique birth and life.

PSALMS OF DEATH'S DEFEAT

> You have made him a little lower than the angels,
> And You have crowned him with glory and
> honor. (Ps. 8:5 NKJV)

Psalm 8 is a profound psalm that considers creation as a work of God's own hands: "When I consider your heavens, the work of your fingers, the moon and the stars, which you have set in place" (v. 3). In view of God's great work as creator, mankind is comparatively insignificant—and yet cherished above all of creation.

The habitation of Christ on earth is compared with the glory He had when He returned to heaven: "You have made him a little lower than the angels, and You have crowned him with glory and honor" (v. 5 NKJV). This revelation is summarized in Hebrews 2:8: "For in that He put all in subjection under him, He left nothing that is not put under him. But now we do not yet see all things put under him" (NKJV). Christ now has not realized subjection of the whole world, suffering death on the cross and being made "perfect through what he suffered" (Heb. 2:10). His right to rule is affirmed: "You have made him to have dominion over the works of Your hands; You have put all things under his feet, all sheep and oxen—even the beasts of the field, the birds of the air, and the fish of the sea that pass through the paths of the seas" (Ps. 8:6–8 NKJV).

The contrast of Psalm 8 was between Christ and Adam. It was God's intent that Adam should rule the world, but this was interrupted by the entrance of sin into the situation. Now Christ has fulfilled what was originally Adam's responsibility. Having suffered on earth and gone through the humiliation of death, Christ now has been exalted to heaven, and it is God's purpose ultimately for Him to rule over the earth.

> My God, my God, why have you forsaken me?
> Why are you so far from saving me,
> so far from my cries of anguish? (Ps. 22:1)

Upon reading Psalm 22, we are reminded that David lived a remarkable life, one of intrigue, despair, and victory. Yet some of the expressions in the psalms go far beyond any sufferings that David himself experienced. There was no known incident in the life of David that corresponded exactly to what this psalm states. What might have been true of David as a type of one suffering was fulfilled literally by the sufferings of Christ. As such, the opening verse of Psalm 22 was quoted by Christ, as recorded in Matthew 27:46 and Mark 15:34.

In his distress, David reassured himself that his God was "enthroned" (Ps. 22:3). People's scorn and mocking and insults mentioned in verses 6–8 were similar to what those who mocked Christ on the cross expressed, not realizing they were quoting Scripture (Matt. 27:39, 42–44). Those who surrounded the cross were compared to bulls and roaring lions (Ps. 22:12–13), and His strength (or "mouth") was "dried up like a potsherd" (v. 15).

This is an obvious reference to the crucifixion: "Dogs surround me, a pack of villains encircles me; they pierce my hands and my feet" (v. 16). The "dogs" were evil people.

Rude stares and the casting of lots for His clothing are described in verses 17–18. David's personal deliverance is indicated in verses 22–24, but it may also refer to Christ in His post-resurrection ministry. The ultimate result is predicted in verses 27–28: "All the ends of the earth will remember and turn to the LORD, and all the families of the nations will bow down before him, for dominion belongs to the LORD and he rules over the nations." The psalm closes in verses 29–31 with a note of victory and praise that refers to David's life, and in the case of Christ, to His post-resurrection triumph.

> Do not turn me over to the desire of my foes,
>   for false witnesses rise up against me,
>   spouting malicious accusations. (Ps. 27:12)

Psalm 27 foreshadows the false witnesses who would be brought against Christ (Matt. 26:59–61; Mark 14:57–59). This theme is also mentioned in Psalm 35:11.

Into your hands I commit my spirit. (Ps. 31:5)

Psalm 31 is another psalm that is not always considered messianic, but Christ precisely repeated the words of verse 5 while on the cross (Luke 23:46). Peter expressed the same thought in 1 Peter 4:19.

He protects all his bones,
    not one of them will be broken. (Ps. 34:20)

Psalm 34 reiterates that God is trustworthy at all times, even down to the smallest detail. In Jesus's brutal death, none of His bones were broken, in contrast with the treatment of the two criminals who were crucified beside Him (John 19:36).

Do not let those gloat over me
    who are my enemies without cause;
do not let those who hate me without reason
    maliciously wink the eye. (Ps. 35:19)

Psalm 35 prophesies that the Savior would be hated without just cause. Indeed, Jesus was hated by those who opposed Him, and this hatred fueled the campaign that called for His death (John 15:24–25; Ps. 69:4).

> My friends and companions avoid me because of
> my wounds;
> my neighbors stay far away. (Ps. 38:11)

In reading Psalm 38, we are reminded that Jesus was friend to
the friendless, a fact that was noted with curiosity. He cared for and
invested in the lives of tax collectors, lepers, and cultural enemies. Yet
in His darkest hour and time of need, Jesus's friends stayed far away.
From the friends who fell asleep when they should have been praying
with Him in the garden of Gethsemane to the friends and family
who watched from a distance as He was crucified and His body taken
away (Matt. 27:55; Mark 15:40; Luke 23:49).

> I do not hide your righteousness in my heart;
> I speak of your faithfulness and your
> saving help.
> I do not conceal your love and your faithfulness
> from the great assembly. (Ps. 40:10)

Psalm 40 is considered a messianic psalm largely because verses
6–8 are quoted in Hebrews 10:5–7 as being fulfilled. As the psalm
states, these verses refer to David's praise to the Lord and his desire
to do the will of God. This, however, also anticipated prophetically
Christ's perfect obedience and His sacrifice as superior to the sacrifices of the Mosaic law. The argument of Hebrews 10 is that Christ
in His perfect sacrifice supplied that which the law could not do
with its temporary sacrifices. Key words in the psalm are *righteousness, faithfulness, saving,* and *love* (v. 10).

> Even my close friend,
>> someone I trusted,
> one who shared my bread,
>> has turned against me. (Ps. 41:9)

The prophecy in Psalm 41 certainly holds true of Christ, who was betrayed by a cherished friend and disciple, Judas.

> They put gall in my food
>> and gave me vinegar for my thirst. (Ps. 69:21)

The portions of Psalm 69 detailing David's cry for help parallel the sufferings of Christ. Those who hated David were similar to those who hated Christ, as verse 4 states: "Those who hate me without reason outnumber the hairs of my head." The zeal of David in verse 9, "for zeal for your house consumes me," was related by the disciples to Christ in explaining Christ's cleansing of the temple (John 2:17).

David's statement that "they put gall in my food and gave me vinegar for my thirst" relates to the vinegar given to Christ on the cross (Matt. 27:48; Mark 15:36; Luke 23:36). Though not a direct prophecy, these passages can be interpreted typically as relating to Christ.

> The stone the builders rejected
>> has become the cornerstone;
> the LORD has done this,
>> and it is marvelous in our eyes.
>> (Ps. 118:22–23)

Psalm 118 is a direct prophecy concerning the Messiah. Christ as the rejected King in His second coming will be the cornerstone; that is, He will fulfill what was anticipated in His authority as King of Kings in ruling the entire earth.

THE PRECIOUS CORNERSTONE

> See, I lay a stone in Zion, a tested stone,
>   a precious cornerstone for a sure
>   foundation. (Isa. 28:16)

In the midst of the statements of coming judgment in Isaiah 28, revelation was given concerning Jesus Christ as "a stone … a sure foundation; the one who relies on it will never be stricken with panic" (v. 16; see also Ps. 118:22–23; Eph. 2:20; 1 Pet. 2:6).

THE SUFFERING SERVANT TO BE EXALTED

> But he was pierced for our transgressions,
>   he was crushed for our iniquities;
> the punishment that brought us peace was on him,
>   and by his wounds we are healed. (Isa. 53:5)

Isaiah 52–53 foretells the suffering Servant's death and glory. In the process of death, the servant of the Lord will suffer (52:14). The result will be, however, that blessings will extend to many nations (v. 15; see also Rom. 15:21).

The great messianic prophecy of Isaiah 53 is devoted to describing the death of Christ. Portions of this section of Isaiah are quoted in the New Testament. Israel's rejection of Jesus was pictured. He had no outward beauty, and He was despised and not esteemed (Isa. 53:2–3). Those in Israel who understood that Christ had died for them recognized that He took their infirmities on Himself (Matt. 8:17). The Servant was afflicted because of Israel's transgressions.

The truth was summarized in Isaiah 53:6: "We all, like sheep, have gone astray, each of us has turned to our own way; and the LORD has laid on him the iniquity of us all." The Servant was compared to a lamb being brought to the slaughter because He did not open His mouth. His death made it impossible for Him to have physical descendants (Acts 8:32–33). His "grave" was "with the wicked" but also "with the rich" (Isa. 53:9; 1 Pet. 2:22). The Servant died in the will of God because "his life" was made "an offering for sin" (Isa. 53:10). This prophecy was fulfilled in Christ's death, with the blessing to be fulfilled in the millennium.

His spiritual offspring would spring from His death and resurrection (Isa. 53:10). His ultimate victory over the wicked is described in verses 11–12 (see also Luke 22:30).

THE PROPHECY IN JONAH

Now the LORD provided a huge fish to swallow Jonah, and Jonah was in the belly of the fish three days and three nights. (Jonah 1:17)

The book of Jonah, probably written by Jonah himself, docu-
ments one of the more familiar stories of the Old Testament. Jonah
described himself only as the son of Amittai from Gath Hepher
(2 Kings 14:25), which was located in Zebulun (Josh. 19:10, 13).

Jonah had received a command to go and preach to Nineveh and
had attempted to flee from the Lord, only to be deterred by a great
storm on a ship bound for Tarshish (probably Spain). After being
rescued by the great fish and cast on shore, he preached his message
to Nineveh, only to be disappointed by her amazing repentance. If
Jonah's ministry occurred about 150 years before the fall of Nineveh
(612 BC), the book records a unique situation in which God spared
a Gentile city for more than a century because of her immediate
repentance in response to the preaching of Jonah.

The book of Jonah, essentially a narrative, contains only a few
prophecies beyond those immediately fulfilled. When the storm
engulfed the ship, Jonah rightly prophesied that if they threw him
overboard, the storm would cease: "'Pick me up and throw me into
the sea,' he replied, 'and it will become calm. I know that it is my
fault that this great storm has come upon you'" (Jonah 1:12). After
initially hesitating to take his life, the sailors threw Jonah overboard.
The sea immediately became calm and was proof to the men that
Jonah's God was real (vv. 15–16).

The prophecy that Nineveh would be destroyed in forty days
was conditional. After her repentance, her judgment was deferred
for 150 years—to Jonah's displeasure. The narrative gives remarkable
insight into Israel's lack of ministry to the Gentile world.

The principal prophetic significance of Jonah, however, was the
fact that Christ Himself referred to Jonah and his experience as a type

of His own death and resurrection as stated in Matthew 12:39–40: "He answered, 'A wicked and adulterous generation asks for a sign! But none will be given it except the sign of the prophet Jonah. For as Jonah was three days and three nights in the belly of a huge fish, so the Son of Man will be three days and three nights in the heart of the earth.'" In this statement, Christ affirmed not only the historicity of Jonah himself but also the historicity of Jonah's strange experience of being swallowed by a great fish and eventually delivered safely to shore.

The question has also been raised as to whether the three days and three nights automatically mean seventy-two hours. Some scholars believe that they may include only parts of three days and that a part of the day was counted as a whole frequently in the Bible. In the traditional view of Christ's crucifixion on Friday, the time span of His resurrection was less than that which was prophesied for Jonah unless it is understood to refer to parts of days. Some explain this by placing the death of Christ on Thursday or Wednesday.

In connection with the unbelief of the Pharisees and Sadducees who were seeking signs, Christ stated, "A wicked and adulterous generation looks for a sign, but none will be given it except the sign of Jonah" (Matt. 16:4; see also Luke 11:29–32).

Though some have doubted the story of Jonah because it was an unusual event—truly supernatural—it is no stranger than many other supernatural acts of God. The events of Jonah must be taken as historical, and their application prophetically by Christ was confirmation of the veracity and inspiration of the book of Jonah. Obviously, additional supernatural factors were at work as the great fish swallowed Jonah and later delivered him to dry land. The major factor of confirmation, however, was the word of Christ Himself that the story of Jonah was true, illustrating the supernatural character of His own death and resurrection.

THE COMING DELIVERANCE OF THE MESSIAH

> See, your king comes to you,
>   righteous and victorious,
> lowly and riding on a donkey,
>   on a colt, the foal of a donkey. (Zech. 9:9)

Zechariah 9:9–17 shows that in contrast to the destruction of the enemies of Israel, Jerusalem would be blessed when her Messiah came. A particular prophecy was given concerning Christ entering Jerusalem in the triumphant procession: "Rejoice greatly, Daughter Zion! Shout, Daughter Jerusalem! See, your king comes to you, righteous and victorious, lowly and riding on a donkey, on a colt, the foal of a donkey" (v. 9). The announcement related to the first coming of Christ (Isa. 9:5–7; Mic. 5:2–4; Luke 1:32–33). His righteous character is revealed in both the Old Testament and the New Testament (Ps. 45:6–7; Isa. 11:1–5; Jer. 23:5–6). He would and yet will come as a deliverer having salvation, both in the sense of providing personal salvation for those who put their trust in Him and ultimately in delivering Israel from their enemies. The prophecy particularly described Christ in His first coming as "lowly and riding on a donkey, on a colt, the foal of a donkey" (Zech. 9:9). This was fulfilled literally as recorded in Matthew 21.

The prophecies that followed blended the first and second comings of Christ as if they were one event (Isa. 9:6–7; 61:1–2; Luke

4:18–21). The prophetic vision extended to the future kingdom on earth: "I will take away the chariots from Ephraim and the warhorses from Jerusalem, and the battle bow will be broken. He will proclaim peace to the nations. His rule will extend from sea to sea and from the River to the ends of the earth" (Zech. 9:10). This was not accomplished in His first coming but will be accomplished in His second coming. The millennial kingdom will be characterized as a time of peace (Isa. 2:4; Mic. 4:3). The nation Israel will occupy the land originally promised to Abram—from the river of Egypt to the Euphrates. The rest of the world will come under the rule of Christ as King of Kings and Lord of Lords.

THE REJECTION OF ISRAEL'S MESSIAH AND ITS CONSEQUENCES

So they paid me thirty pieces of silver. (Zech. 11:12)

Though scriptures preceding Zechariah 11 had anticipated the ultimate restoration of Israel, the long process before this was fulfilled as it pointed to the rejection of the Messiah. As such, the cedars of Lebanon, the oaks of Bashan, and the rich pastures of the land were all to be destroyed (vv. 1–3).

Zechariah was told to assume the role of a shepherd and pasture the flock of Israel. The religious leaders of Israel, represented by Zechariah, were not true shepherds and did not care for the sheep but instead would oppress them (vv. 4–6).

Acting the part of a shepherd, Zechariah took two staffs called Favor and Union (v. 7). It is not clear what Scripture means when

THE MISSION OF THE MESSIAH

it states, "In one month I got rid of the three shepherds" (v. 8). The leaders of Israel occupied the offices of prophet, priest, and king, and it is possible it referred to this.

The flock, however, would not receive Zechariah as her shepherd. Accordingly, he broke the staff Favor, indicating that she no longer was in favor with God. As a shepherd, he asked for his pay (v. 12). Scripture records, "So they paid me thirty pieces of silver" (v. 12). This was the price of a slave, but Zechariah, acting the role of the shepherd, threw the thirty pieces of silver into the house of the Lord for the potter (v. 13). He then broke the second staff called Union, representing the brotherly relation between Judah and Israel, already fractured into two kingdoms. This anticipated prophetically that Judas would be paid thirty pieces of silver to betray Christ (Matt. 26:14–16; 27:3–10).

Zechariah was then told to take the role of a foolish shepherd (Zech. 11:15), representing prophetically the Antichrist, who will lead Israel in the end time. Woe was pronounced on this restless shepherd (v. 17).

While not all of the prophetic details in this chapter are clear, it generally indicates the reason why Israel's restoration did not take place sooner and points to her rejection of the Messiah in His first coming. Despite this rejection, it was God's settled purpose to enthrone Christ as the King of Israel. The statement of this purpose of God was set in the context of the military conflict that will precede His coming.

THE PROPHECY OF THE TRUE PROPHET

> Strike the shepherd,
> and the sheep will be scattered. (Zech. 13:7)

In Zechariah 13:7–9, the true Shepherd was declared to be struck, with the result that the sheep were scattered (v. 7). This was fulfilled in the crucifixion of Christ, whose disciples were confused and lost in the days following His death. Following His resurrection, His disciples were indeed scattered, as they spread to the far corners of the earth to share the good news.

5

ONE IN A MILLION: HOW JESUS'S LIFE FULFILLED ANCIENT PROPHECIES

How could one person fulfill hundreds of prophecies that had been specifically and precisely told about Him long before His birth? For the typical person, that would be completely impossible. But for someone who is the Son of God sent to earth to live as a human being, that is entirely possible.

In fact, Jesus Himself said, "I am telling you now before it happens, so that when it does happen you will believe that I am who I am. Very truly I tell you, whoever accepts anyone I send accepts me; and whoever accepts me accepts the one who sent me" (John 13:19–20). It's no wonder that Jesus referred to ancient prophecies, provided prophecies of His own, and completed numerous prophecies about Himself. What follows is a sample of the prophecies fulfilled by Christ.

JESUS AS THE SON OF DAVID

> This is the genealogy of Jesus the Messiah the son of David, the son of Abraham. (Matt. 1:1)

The gospel of Matthew is unique in presenting both the life of Christ from a particular point of view and an explanation of why the Old Testament prophecies concerning the kingdom on earth were not fulfilled at the first coming of Christ. Unlike the gospel of Luke, which is designed to set forth an accurate historical record of the facts concerning Christ (Luke 1:1–4), the gospel of Matthew has the specific purpose of explaining to Jews, who expected their Messiah to be a conquering and glorious king, why Christ instead lived among men and women, died on a cross, and rose again. In keeping with this objective, the gospel of Matthew provides a bridge between the Old Testament prophecies and expectation of the coming of the Messiah of Israel and its fulfillment in the birth and life of Christ.

As such, Matthew 1:1–17 traces back the lineage of Jesus to Abraham and David. The genealogy ends with Joseph, the husband of Mary. Matthew made clear that Jesus was not the son of Joseph but that Mary was His mother (Matt. 1:16). By contrast, the genealogy of Mary is given in Luke 3:23–38, assuring that Christ is a genuine descendant of David. The genealogy of Matthew supports the concept that Jesus is the legitimate heir to the throne of David through Joseph His father. Even though Joseph was not the human father of Jesus, the right of the royal throne was nevertheless passed through Joseph to Jesus. Therefore, Jesus fulfilled the Old Testament expectation that a son of David would reign on the throne of David forever, as Gabriel had announced to Mary (Luke 1:32–33).

A careful study of Matthew's genealogy reveals that it was not intended to be a complete genealogy, as only fourteen generations were selected from Abraham to David, fourteen from David to the Babylonian exile, and fourteen from the exile to the time of Jesus's birth. Matthew 1:13–15 records people in the genealogy of Jesus who are not listed in the Old Testament. Likewise, some names in the Old Testament are not included in the genealogy as in the case of Uzziah, who was declared to be the son of Jehoram when actually he was the great-great-grandson of Jehoram (Matt. 1:8; 2 Kings 8:25; 13:1–15:38; 2 Chron. 22–25).

The fact that the New Testament includes some names not in the Old Testament and the Old Testament includes some names not in the New Testament is one of the reasons why it is impossible to take genealogies as a basis for determining the antiquity of the human race, as the Scriptures themselves make plain that this was not the divine intent. On the other hand, it does not justify the point of view that the human race is many thousands of years older than the Scriptures seem to indicate.

Another unusual feature of the genealogies is the prominence of four women who would not normally be included in a genealogy. Each of them has a special background. Tamar (Matt. 1:3) actually got into the line by playing the harlot (Gen. 38). Rahab the harlot was protected by Joshua when Jericho was captured and became part of the messianic line (Josh. 2:1–6; 6:25). Rahab was declared to be the wife of Salmon, the father of Boaz, and this was revealed only in the New Testament (Matt. 1:5). Only Ruth, the subject of a beautiful portrayal in the book that bears her name, had an unspotted record; but even she was not an Israelite. Bathsheba the mother of Solomon, who had formerly been the wife of Uriah, had an adulterous relationship with David that resulted in the murder of her husband (2 Sam. 11–12). The fact that these women were in the genealogy also put a stop to any Jewish pride. Undoubtedly,

Mary also had to withstand the burden of gossip concerning her son, who was conceived before she became Joseph's bride.

THE BIRTH OF JESUS

> You will conceive and give birth to a son, and you are to call him Jesus. He will be great and will be called the Son of the Most High. The Lord God will give him the throne of his father David, and he will reign over Jacob's descendants forever; his kingdom will never end. (Luke 1:31–33)

In Luke 1:26–38 we see that just as the angel Gabriel had appeared to Zechariah, six months later he appeared to Mary, described as "a virgin pledged to be married to a man named Joseph, a descendant of David" (v. 27).

The angel greeted her: "Greetings, you who are highly favored! The Lord is with you" (v. 28).

Because Mary was troubled by this greeting, Scripture records the angel's announcement to her: "But the angel said to her, 'Do not be afraid, Mary; you have found favor with God. You will conceive and give birth to a son, and you are to call him Jesus. He will be great and will be called the Son of the Most High. The Lord God will give him the throne of his father David, and he will reign over Jacob's descendants forever; his kingdom will never end'" (vv. 30–33).

The prophecy was too extensive for her to grasp immediately. She probably could not comprehend why He should be called Jesus, which means "savior." He also was to be "Son of the Most High"

(v. 32), meaning that He would be the Son of God. Though Mary was acquainted with the hope of Israel for a messiah and a redeemer, it is undoubtedly true that she did not comprehend completely the fact that her son would have the throne of His father David, that He would reign over this kingdom forever, and that His kingdom would never end (Ps. 89:36; Jer. 23:5–8). Only time would let her contemplate the full extent of the prophecy.

She was concerned, however, with the question as to how she would have a child when she was not yet married. Not surprisingly, Mary asked the angel, "How will this be … since I am a virgin?" (Luke 1:34).

The angel responded, "The Holy Spirit will come on you, and the power of the Most High will overshadow you. So the holy one to be born will be called the Son of God. Even Elizabeth your relative is going to have a child in her old age, and she who was said to be unable to conceive is in her sixth month. For no word from God will ever fail" (vv. 35–37).

Mary's simple response was, "I am the Lord's servant … May your word to me be fulfilled" (v. 38).

Most of the prophecies itemized by Gabriel were fulfilled in the lifetime of Christ. The prophecy concerning Christ's reign on the throne of David is related eschatologically to the second coming of Christ when the Davidic kingdom will be revived and will continue in some form forever.

Of particular importance to end times events is the fact that Christ was predicted to reign on the throne of David. Because many have attempted to limit the prophecy of the Davidic kingdom to the Old Testament and to claim that the New Testament interprets the prophecy in a nonliteral sense as being fulfilled today, this is an important interpretive passage in the New Testament, reaffirming that the Davidic kingdom would be restored literally. This announcement established the hope of the revival of the Davidic kingdom as a New Testament prophecy and gave a basis for a belief in the premillennial return of Christ to be followed by the millennial kingdom and the Davidic kingdom.

Apparently, the Davidic kingdom will be an aspect of the millennial kingdom of Christ and will concern Israel and her regathered situation in the Promised Land. Mary had the expectation, as did the people of Israel, of a future messiah who would literally revive the Davidic kingdom. The angel confirmed this by asserting that Christ would reign on the throne of David. The literal political revival of Israel in relation to the second coming of Christ is not an erroneous interpretation into which the people of Israel had fallen but rather precisely what the Old Testament predicted and what the New Testament here confirms.

ELIZABETH'S PROPHECY CONCERNING JESUS

> Blessed are you among women, and blessed is the
> child you will bear! (Luke 1:42)

In Luke 1:39–45, when Mary realized she was pregnant, she left Nazareth to visit Zechariah's wife. Upon her arrival in Zechariah's home, further confirmation of the angel's message to Mary was recorded: "When Elizabeth heard Mary's greeting, the baby leaped in her womb, and Elizabeth was filled with the Holy Spirit. In a loud voice she exclaimed: 'Blessed are you among women, and blessed is the child you will bear!'" (vv. 41–42).

Elizabeth continued, "But why am I so favored, that the mother of my Lord should come to me? As soon as the sound of your greeting reached my ears, the baby in my womb leaped for joy. Blessed is she who has believed that the Lord would fulfill his promises to her!" (vv. 43–45).

MARY'S SONG OF PRAISE

> [God] has helped his servant Israel,
>   remembering to be merciful
> to Abraham and his descendants forever,
>   just as he promised our ancestors.
>   (Luke 1:54–55)

In Luke 1:46–56, Mary was greatly reassured by the greeting of Elizabeth, which at once confirmed the prophecies concerning John and the prophecies concerning Jesus. In reply, Mary delivered a prophetic poem, often called the "Magnificat":

> My soul glorifies the Lord
>   and my spirit rejoices in God my Savior,
> for he has been mindful
>   of the humble state of his servant.
> From now on all generations will call me blessed,
>   for the Mighty One has done great things
>   for me—
>   holy is his name.

His mercy extends to those who fear him,
> from generation to generation.

He has performed mighty deeds with his arm;
> he has scattered those who are proud in their
> > inmost thoughts.

He has brought down rulers from their thrones
> but has lifted up the humble.

He has filled the hungry with good things
> but has sent the rich away empty.

He has helped his servant Israel,
> remembering to be merciful

to Abraham and his descendants forever,
> just as he promised our ancestors. (vv. 46–55)

Mary's declaration was no doubt inspired by the Holy Spirit, but it also revealed an amazing spiritual maturity for a young woman and an intelligent faith in God that comprehended both the historic and the prophetic aspects of her experience. In her pronouncement, Mary stated that her rejoicing was in God because He had taken her from her humble state and now all generations would call her blessed. She stated that God's mercy extended to those who fear Him and that God performs mighty deeds, bringing down rulers and establishing others. He has filled the hungry and sent the rich away. Most important, He has remembered His promises to Abraham and his descendants. In this declaration Mary was calling attention to the fact that prophecies concerning Abraham and the Davidic kingdom may be expected to have literal fulfillment.

Mary stayed with Elizabeth until just before the birth of John
and then returned to Nazareth.

ZECHARIAH'S PROPHETIC SONG

> [God] has raised up a horn of salvation for us
>   in the house of his servant David.
>   (Luke 1:69)

In Luke 1:68–79, Zechariah, being filled with the Holy Spirit,
delivered his prophetic message:

> Praise be to the Lord, the God of Israel,
>   because he has come to his people and
>   redeemed them.
> He has raised up a horn of salvation for us
>   in the house of his servant David
> (as he said through his holy prophets of long ago),
> salvation from our enemies
>   and from the hand of all who hate us—
> to show mercy to our ancestors
>   and to remember his holy covenant,
>   the oath he swore to our father Abraham:
> to rescue us from the hand of our enemies,
>   and to enable us to serve him without fear
>   in holiness and righteousness before him all of
>   our days.

And you, my child, will be called a prophet of the
    Most High;
  for you will go on before the Lord to prepare the
    way for him,
to give his people the knowledge of salvation
  through the forgiveness of their sins,
because of the tender mercy of our God,
  by which the rising sun will come to us from heaven
to shine on those living in darkness
  and in the shadow of death,
to guide our feet into the path of peace.

In his prophecy, Zechariah, referring to Christ, declared that God had raised up someone to bring deliverance through the house of David. He pointed out that the coming of Christ was in fulfillment of God's solemn oath to Abraham (v. 73).

In regard to John, Zechariah predicted, "And you, my child, will be called a prophet of the Most High" (v. 76). Zechariah also predicted that John would serve as the forerunner to prepare the way for Christ (vv. 76–79). The prophecies through Zechariah, Elizabeth, and Mary were clearly a confirmation of the expectation of the Jews that a son of David would literally appear and would literally deliver His people from their enemies and bring great blessing and salvation to Israel.

THE CONCEPTION AND BIRTH OF JESUS

What is conceived in her is from the Holy Spirit.
She will give birth to a son, and you are to give him

the name Jesus, because he will save his people from
their sins. (Matt. 1:20–21)

In Matthew 1:18–25, when Mary returned from her visit
to Elizabeth, she apparently was three months pregnant, and this
became evident to Joseph. Not willing to make a public example
(and spectacle) of Mary, he had in mind to divorce her quietly.
Matthew explained, however, that God communicated to Joseph the
facts in the case, declaring, "An angel of the Lord appeared to him
in a dream and said, 'Joseph son of David, do not be afraid to take
Mary home as your wife, because what is conceived in her is from
the Holy Spirit. She will give birth to a son, and you are to give him
the name Jesus, because he will save his people from their sins'" (vv.
20–21). Matthew stated that this was in fulfillment of the prophecy
of Isaiah 7:14: "All this took place to fulfill what the Lord had said
through the prophet: 'The virgin will conceive and give birth to a
son, and they will call him Immanuel' (which means, 'God with us')"
(Matt. 1:22–23).

The Scriptures are silent concerning Mary's anxiety in this whole
situation as, apparently, she did not feel free to divulge to Joseph the
facts in the situation. Having received this instruction from God,
however, Joseph "did what the angel of the Lord had commanded
him and took Mary home as his wife. But he did not consummate
their marriage until she gave birth to a son. And he gave him the
name Jesus" (vv. 24–25). No doubt, both Joseph and Mary suffered
malicious gossip concerning this whole matter and were unable to
proclaim the truth. For Mary it was a great relief, however, to have
Joseph take her home as his wife.

THE VISIT OF THE MAGI

> Where is the one who has been born king of the
> Jews? (Matt. 2:2)

In Matthew 2:1–18, the final immediate confirmation of the birth of Jesus as the future King of the Jews came from the visit of the magi, who traveled all the way from Persia to find Jesus. The magi were known as people who studied the stars, and it was possible that they saw the light attending the glorious announcement of the angels. They were not without some information about the Messiah, as there had been frequent contact between Jews and Persians in the years before the birth of Christ, and the idea that Israel was looking forward to a Messiah was apparently widely known.

There is no indication that the number of magi was limited to three, nor that they were kings, though this is often the way they are referred to traditionally. They probably were a larger company. They had apparently sensed what had happened when Christ was born, and it took some months for them to organize and come to Israel to find the baby Jesus. Because Jerusalem was the center of Jewish religion, the magi came asking, "Where is the one who has been born king of the Jews? We saw his star when it rose and have come to worship him" (v. 2). King Herod was much disturbed by this announcement, as he saw the birth of a child destined to be king of the Jews as competition for his own rule. Accordingly, he called the leaders of Israel together to find out where Christ was to be born (vv. 3–4). They replied that He would be born in

Bethlehem of Judea and quoted Micah 5:2 in support of their conclusion (Matt. 2:5–6). King Herod then attempted to discover when the star appeared to determine the time of the child's birth. He told the magi to report to him when they found the child (vv. 7–8).

As the magi journeyed to Bethlehem, the star reappeared and led them to the place where the child was. This time it was not a manger but a house, and it is apparent, taking the whole narrative into consideration, that some weeks, if not months, had passed since the birth of Christ. The magi were overjoyed when they saw Mary and the child and worshipped Him (vv. 9–11). In recognition of the honored child, they brought gifts of gold, frankincense, and myrrh (v. 11). Though they likely were not conscious of the meaning of the gifts, the gold represented the deity of Christ; frankincense, the fragrance of His life; and myrrh, His sacrifice and death. The magi were warned in a dream not to return to Herod (v. 12).

The Lord appeared to Joseph in a dream and told him to take the child and Mary to Egypt because of Herod's plot to kill Jesus (vv. 13–14). Matthew noted that this was a fulfillment of prophecy: "Out of Egypt I called my son" (v. 15; Hosea 11:1). Like the nation as a whole, Christ came out of Egypt to come back to the Promised Land.

When Herod realized that the magi were not going to report to him, he was very angry and ordered that all boys two years old and under in the Bethlehem area be killed. This resulted in the fulfillment of Jeremiah's prophecy: "A voice is heard in Ramah, weeping and great mourning, Rachel weeping for her children and refusing to be comforted, because they are no more" (v. 18; Jer. 31:15).

JOHN THE BAPTIST AS A FORERUNNER OF CHRIST

> I baptize you with water for repentance. But after
> me comes one who is more powerful than I, whose
> sandals I am not worthy to carry. He will baptize
> you with the Holy Spirit and fire. (Matt. 3:11)

Matthew 3:1–12 gives us a look into John the Baptist's preaching that prepared the way for Christ. For four hundred years before John began his prophetic ministry in the wilderness of Judea, there had been no prophet in Israel. Many in Judea and Jerusalem went out to hear him. John himself made a spectacular appearance, living in rough clothing of camels' hair with a leather belt about his waist. His food was locusts and wild honey. His message was abrupt and unyielding; he urged the people to confess their sins (Matt. 3:6; Mark 1:5), and he denounced their religious leaders, especially the Pharisees and the Sadducees, calling them a "brood of vipers!" (Matt. 3:7). His message was one of repentance and baptism with water as a sign of their spiritual change. John predicted that after him would come the prophesied One, "whose sandals I am not worthy to carry" (v. 11).

His message was a practical one. "Anyone who has two shirts should share" (Luke 3:11), and the people should do likewise with their surplus of food. Publicans were exhorted not to extort taxes but only take what was legal. Soldiers were told not to do that which was violent and not to falsely accuse others (vv. 13–14). Matthew, Mark, and Luke each viewed John as fulfilling the prophecies of

Isaiah 40:3: "A voice of one calling in the wilderness, 'Prepare the way for the Lord, make straight paths for him'" (Matt. 3:3; Mark 1:3; Luke 3:4). Though John the Baptist knew Jesus as an individual, he probably did not know that Jesus was the prophesied Messiah until Jesus presented Himself for baptism. John made it clear that he was not the Messiah, but he also anticipated that the true Messiah might appear at any time.

JESUS BAPTIZED BY JOHN IN THE JORDAN

> A voice from heaven said, "This is my Son, whom
> I love; with him I am well pleased." (Matt. 3:17)

In Matthew 3:13–17, when John demurred at the thought of baptizing Jesus, he nevertheless was exhorted to do so. After Jesus was baptized, Matthew, Mark, and Luke all recorded the voice from heaven declaring that Jesus was the beloved Son of the Father. Luke declared that at Jesus's baptism the Holy Spirit descended on Him as a dove and the voice speaking from heaven was God the Father, a clear indication of the Trinity: the Father, Son, and Holy Spirit. The commendation of Jesus by God the Father was anticipated in Psalm 2:7 and Isaiah 42:1.

JESUS IN HIS HEALING MINISTRY WOULD FULFILL PROPHECY

> Here is my servant whom I have chosen,
> the one I love, in whom I delight. (Matt. 12:18)

Matthew 12:9–20 shows Jesus as a healing servant and thus fulfilling God's prophecy. Because Jesus had healed on the Sabbath, the Pharisees plotted to kill Him (vv. 9–14). Knowing of their plots to kill Him, Jesus told the people He healed to keep silent about His miracles, thus fulfilling Isaiah 42:1–4.

> Aware of this, Jesus withdrew from that place. A large crowd followed him, and he healed all who were ill. He warned them not to tell others about him. This was to fulfill what was spoken through the prophet Isaiah:
>
> "Here is my servant whom I have chosen,
>   the one I love, in whom I delight;
> I will put my Spirit on him,
>   and he will proclaim justice to the nations.
> He will not quarrel or cry out;
>   no one will hear his voice in the streets.
> A bruised reed he will not break,
>   and a smoldering wick he will not snuff out,
> till he has brought justice through victory."
>   (Matt. 12:15–20)

As Isaiah prophesied, Jesus was a delight to God the Father, beloved and indwelt by the Holy Spirit. He would proclaim justice but would not quarrel or cry out. His would ultimately be the victory (vv. 18–20).

JESUS AS THE GOOD SHEPHERD

> I am the good shepherd. The good shepherd lays
> down his life for the sheep. (John 10:11)

In John 10:1–18, Jesus expanded on the fact that He was the Good Shepherd and that His sheep would follow Him. In verse 5, He said, "But they will never follow a stranger; in fact, they will run away from him because they do not recognize a stranger's voice." When the disciples did not understand this, Jesus enlarged the explanation by declaring, "Very truly I tell you, I am the gate for the sheep. All who have come before me are thieves and robbers, but the sheep have not listened to them. I am the gate; whoever enters through me will be saved. They will come in and go out, and find pasture. The thief comes only to steal and kill and destroy; I have come that they may have life, and have it to the full" (vv. 7–10). Jesus was declaring that He is the only Savior and that those who are saved through Him will not only have life but will also have pasture and God's care. They will have life and have life to the full (v. 10).

In further elaborating on the declaration that He was the Good Shepherd, Jesus declared, "I am the good shepherd. The good shepherd lays down his life for the sheep" (v. 11). In contrast to false shepherds who flee when the wolf comes and abandon the sheep (vv. 12–13), Jesus said, "I am the good shepherd; I know my sheep and my sheep know me—just as the Father knows me and I know the Father—and I lay down my life for the sheep" (vv. 14–15). As the Good Shepherd in dying on the cross, Jesus died for His sheep.

In proclaiming that He was the Good Shepherd, Jesus added, "I have other sheep that are not of this sheep pen. I must bring them also. They too will listen to my voice, and there shall be one flock and one shepherd" (v. 16). In this prophecy Jesus was anticipating the church, comprising both Jews and Gentiles, in which the wall of partition between would be broken down and they would be one in Christ, be one flock and have one shepherd.

Jesus then enlarged on His sacrifice of His life, declaring, "The reason my Father loves me is that I lay down my life—only to take it up again. No one takes it from me, but I lay it down of my own accord. I have authority to lay it down and authority to take it up again. This command I received from my Father" (vv. 17–18). In making this assertion, Jesus was anticipating His death on the cross when He would lay down His life for the sheep. In the case of Jesus, however, He not only had the power to lay down His life, but He also had the power to take it up again—something that had never been true of any previous person raised from the dead. This was to be the supreme proof of His deity, which His disciples recognized. As a study of Christ's resurrection demonstrates, Jesus was not simply restored to the life He had before His death, but He was also given a new body, the pattern of the resurrection body of the saints that they will receive at the time of the resurrection or rapture.

6

JESUS'S PREDICTIONS: PROPHECIES THAT JESUS HIMSELF GAVE US

Throughout the course of His ministry, Jesus blessed the people through His teachings, many of which were antithetical to the popular teachings of the day. Jesus also prophesied about the trajectory of the world and the path that His followers would take until His second coming.

THE PROPHETIC CHARACTER OF THE BEATITUDES

> Blessed are the poor in spirit. (Matt. 5:3)

Matthew 5:1–12 contains the beatitudes, which are a good illustration of the ethical character of the kingdom, including present blessing but also future reward. Each of the beatitudes speaks of present blessing and then the ultimate blessing in the kingdom. Accordingly, those who are "poor in spirit" will possess "the kingdom of heaven" (v. 3). Those who "mourn" are promised "they will be comforted" (v. 4). Those who are "the meek" are promised "they will inherit the earth" (v. 5). Those at the present time "who hunger and thirst for righteousness" are promised "they will be filled" (v. 6). Those who are "merciful" will have mercy shown to them (v. 7). Those who are "pure in heart" are promised "they will see God" (v. 8). Those who are "the peacemakers" are promised they "will be called children of God" (v. 9). Those who are "persecuted because of righteousness" are promised "theirs is the kingdom of heaven" (v. 10). These beatitudes are general in their promise to anyone who qualifies.

Immediately following these beatitudes, Jesus made an application to the disciples themselves. He declared, "Blessed are you when people insult you, persecute you and falsely say all kinds of evil against you because of me. Rejoice and be glad, because great is your reward in heaven, for in the same way they persecuted the prophets who were before you" (vv. 11–12). What is true of the beatitudes is true of other promises in the Sermon on the Mount. There is present application, and there is future promise of reward.

THE LAW AND THE PROPHECIES TO BE FULFILLED IN THE FUTURE KINGDOM

> Do not think that I have come to abolish the Law or the Prophets; I have not come to abolish them but to fulfill them. For truly I tell you, until heaven and earth disappear, not the smallest letter, not the least stroke of a pen, will by any means disappear from the Law until everything is accomplished. (Matt. 5:17–18)

Matthew 5:17–20 addresses prophecies related to the fulfillment of the law. The dispensation of the Mosaic law was to be brought to its end in the earth by Christ, but its end would not be one of being abolished but one of being fulfilled. Accordingly, as Paul wrote in 2 Corinthians 3:13, the radiance of the law "was passing away." Likewise, the Galatians were instructed, "Now that the way of faith has come, we no longer need the law as our guardian" (Gal. 3:25 NLT). The Mosaic law was limited in its application to the nation of Israel and was limited as to its continuance because it was to be fulfilled by Christ and succeeded by another dispensation.

The spiritual and moral principles of the law, however, continue, and Jesus declared, "For truly I tell you, until heaven and earth disappear, not the smallest letter, not the least stroke of a pen, will by any means disappear from the Law until everything is accomplished" (Matt. 5:18). Accordingly, though the Mosaic law as a direct application was terminated, the moral and spiritual principles involved were to continue forever. In this statement, Jesus was affirming the inspiration of Scripture extending not simply to the words but also to the smallest letter or the smallest part of a letter. The smallest Hebrew letter was *yod*, and the smallest part of a letter was probably a tittle, which refers to the smallest part of a lettering being changed and affecting its meaning. An illustration in English is provided in the English capital letter *E*. If the bottom horizontal line is removed, it becomes a capital *F*. In the letter *E*, the tittle is the bottom horizontal line.

Building on this revelation, Jesus declared that breaking the commandments and teaching others to do the same would call for judgment, resulting in some not entering the kingdom. On the other hand, those who obey the law and the moral principles of the kingdom "will be called great in the kingdom of heaven" (Matt. 5:19).

TRUE BELIEVERS IN JESUS TO ENTER THE KINGDOM OF HEAVEN

> Go! Let it be done just as you believed it would.
> (Matt. 8:13)

In Matthew 8:5–13, when Jesus entered Capernaum, a centurion approached Him, asking Him to heal his servant who was in terrible suffering at his home. Jesus responded that He would go heal him (vv. 5–7). The centurion replied, however, that it was not necessary for Him to go because He could command, just as the centurion commanded his soldiers to do things, and it would be done (vv. 8–9).

The Scriptures record:

> When Jesus heard this, he was amazed and said to those following him, "Truly I tell you, I have not found anyone in Israel with such great faith. I say to you that many will come from the east and the west, and will take their places at the feast with Abraham, Isaac and Jacob in the kingdom of heaven. But the subjects of the kingdom will be thrown outside, into the darkness, where there will be weeping and gnashing of teeth." (vv. 10–12)

The story concludes with Jesus telling the centurion, "'Go! Let it be done just as you believed it would.' And his servant was healed at that moment" (v. 13).

JESUS'S PREDICTION OF THE BUILDING OF HIS CHURCH

> I tell you that you are Peter, and on this rock I will
> build my church, and the gates of Hades will not
> overcome it. (Matt. 16:18)

In Matthew 16:17–19, His first prediction concerning the future church, Jesus declared that it would be built on Peter in the sense that the apostle would belong to the first generation of Christians. Furthermore, Jesus would give to Peter and the other disciples the keys of the kingdom of heaven, which was the message of the gospel that through Christ they could enter the kingdom of heaven (vv. 18–19).

PROMISE TO ANSWER PRAYER

> Again, truly I tell you that if two of you on earth
> agree about anything they ask for, it will be done
> for them by my Father in heaven. (Matt. 18:19)

Matthew 18:19–20 proclaims if two agree on earth concerning a prayer request, their prayer will be answered. Best of all, wherever a gathering assembles in the name of Christ, Jesus Himself will be present among them.

THE FIRST PREDICTIONS OF HIS DEATH AND RESURRECTION

> From that time on Jesus began to explain to his disciples that he must go to Jerusalem and suffer many things at the hands of the elders, the chief priests and the teachers of the law, and that he must be killed and on the third day be raised to life. (Matt. 16:21)

In Matthew 16:21–28, Jesus predicted His coming death and resurrection. Though Peter objected strenuously, Jesus rebuked him and reminded him and the other disciples that there was a cross to be taken up in following Him. The principle is: "For whoever wants to save their life will lose it, but whoever loses their life for me will find it" (v. 25). Though He would need to die and be resurrected, He would return in power and glory from heaven (v. 27), and He also predicted that some of the disciples would not die before they saw "the Son of Man coming in his kingdom" (v. 28). This is most probably a reference to the transfiguration, which took place immediately afterward when Jesus was revealed in the glory that will be His.

THE SECOND PROPHECY OF JESUS CONCERNING HIS DEATH AND RESURRECTION

> On the third day he will be raised to life! (Matt. 20:19)

The second prediction of Christ concerning His death and resurrection is recorded in three of the gospels (Matt. 20:17–19; Mark 10:32–34; Luke 18:31–34). The twelve disciples were on their way to Jerusalem, and Jesus took them away from the multitude and told them, "We are going up to Jerusalem, and the Son of Man will be delivered over to the chief priests and the teachers of the law. They will condemn him to death and will hand him over to the Gentiles to be mocked and flogged and crucified. On the third day he will be raised to life!" (Matt. 20:18–19).

Luke added, "The disciples did not understand any of this. Its meaning was hidden from them, and they did not know what he was talking about" (Luke 18:34).

A THIRD ANNOUNCEMENT OF THE DEATH AND RESURRECTION OF JESUS

The Son of Man will be handed over to be crucified.
(Matt. 26:2)

In Matthew 26:2–5, the third announcement of Christ's death, Jesus did not mention the fact that He would also be raised from the dead. Luke 22:1–6 adds more information about the plot of Judas to betray Jesus to the chief priests at an opportune time.

JESUS PREDICTS HIS DEATH AND RESURRECTION

To those who sold doves [Jesus] said, "Get these out of here! Stop turning my Father's house into a market!"

> His disciples remembered that it is written: "Zeal for
> your house will consume me." (John 2:16–17)

John 2:13–22 records Jesus's first purification of the temple. Jesus had driven the sheep and the cattle out of the temple area and scattered the tables of the money changers (v. 15). John 2 continues, however, "The Jews then responded to him, 'What sign can you show us to prove your authority to do all this?'" (v. 18). Jesus's reply was the prediction of His death and resurrection: "Destroy this temple, and I will raise it again in three days" (v. 19).

The Jews, of course, thought He was talking about the temple that Herod was building, which had been under construction for forty-six years (v. 20). John 2 explains that the temple Jesus was talking about was His body (v. 21). At the time, the disciples did not understand what Jesus had said, but "after he was raised from the dead, his disciples recalled what he had said. Then they believed the scripture and the words that Jesus had spoken" (v. 22).

THE PROPHECIES OF JESUS AT THE LAST PASSOVER FEAST

> [The disciples] were very sad and began to say to
> [Jesus] one after the other, "Surely you don't mean
> me, Lord?" (Matt. 26:22)

Matthew 26:17–75 provides a number of prophecies in connection with the last twenty-four hours of Jesus's life on earth prior to

His crucifixion. Jesus announced that one of His disciples would betray Him: "Truly I tell you, one of you will betray me" (v. 21). When each of them denied this, Jesus replied, "The one who has dipped his hand into the bowl with me will betray me. The Son of Man will go just as it is written about him. But woe to that man who betrays the Son of Man! It would be better for him if he had not been born" (vv. 23–24). After this prediction, the Scriptures recorded that "Judas, the one who would betray him, said, 'Surely you don't mean me, Rabbi?' Jesus answered, 'You have said so'" (v. 25). Later that night, Judas betrayed Jesus.

While they were observing the institution of the Lord's Supper at the time of the Passover feast, Jesus declared, "I tell you, I will not drink from this fruit of the vine from now on until that day when I drink it new with you in my Father's kingdom" (v. 29). Jesus was referring to the millennial kingdom when they would again be together following their resurrection.

After they had left the upper room and had gone on their way to the Mount of Olives, Jesus said to them, "This very night you will all fall away on account of me, for it is written: 'I will strike the shepherd, and the sheep of the flock will be scattered.' But after I have risen, I will go ahead of you into Galilee" (vv. 31–32). When Peter denied that he would do this, Jesus said, "Truly I tell you … this very night, before the rooster crows, you will disown me three times" (v. 34; see also Mark 14:29–31; Luke 22:34; John 13:35–38). This prophecy, accordingly, was fulfilled later that night as well as the prophecy that all the disciples would flee.

In connection with His questioning before the Sanhedrin, Jesus was asked by the high priest, "I charge you under oath by the living

God: Tell us if you are the Messiah, the Son of God" (Matt. 26:63). "Jesus said to him, 'It is as you said. Nevertheless, I say to you, hereafter you will see the Son of Man sitting at the right hand of the Power, and coming on the clouds of heaven'" (v. 64 NKJV). The high priest took this as the same as claiming to be God and declared Him worthy of death (vv. 65–66).

JESUS WILL LEAVE BUT SEND THE SPIRIT

> On the last and greatest day of the festival, Jesus stood and said in a loud voice, "Let anyone who is thirsty come to me and drink. Whoever believes in me, as Scripture has said, rivers of living water will flow from within them." (John 7:37–38)

In John 7:25–39, as the people were puzzled that Jesus had not been arrested, guards were sent from the temple to take Him into custody. Jesus told the guards sent to arrest Him, "I am with you for only a short time, and then I am going to the one who sent me. You will look for me, but you will not find me; and where I am, you cannot come" (vv. 33–34).

John then recorded Jesus's prediction of the coming of the Holy Spirit:

> Jesus stood and said in a loud voice, "Let anyone who is thirsty come to me and drink. Whoever believes in me, as Scripture has said, rivers of living water will flow from within them." By this he

meant the Spirit, whom those who believed in him were later to receive. Up to that time the Spirit had not been given, since Jesus had not yet been glorified. (vv. 37–39)

In His prediction, Jesus anticipated the coming of the Spirit on the day of Pentecost and the Holy Spirit filling the disciples.

JESUS PREDICTS HIS BETRAYAL BY JUDAS, HIS DENIAL BY PETER, AND HIS DEPARTURE

I am telling you now before it happens, so that when it does happen you will believe that I am who I am. (John 13:19)

John 13:18–38 covers Judas's betrayal and Peter's denial. After referring to the importance of accepting Him, Jesus said plainly, "Very truly I tell you, one of you is going to betray me" (John 13:21). The disciples did not know what to do about this statement (v. 22). But John the beloved disciple, who apparently was next to Christ at the table, asked Jesus, "Lord, who is it?" (v. 25). Jesus answered, "'It is the one to whom I will give this piece of bread when I have dipped it in the dish.' Then, dipping the piece of bread, he gave it to Judas, the son of Simon Iscariot. As soon as Judas took the bread, Satan entered into him" (vv. 26–27).

Apparently, only John the apostle knew of the identification of Judas Iscariot as the one who would betray Jesus. Judas himself, after he had taken the bread, went out (v. 30). Jesus then announced to His disciples, "Now the Son of Man is glorified and God is glorified in him. If God is glorified in him, God will glorify the Son in himself, and will glorify him at once" (vv. 31–32).

Jesus declared that He was not going to be with them much longer. He said, "My children, I will be with you only a little longer. You will look for me, and just as I told the Jews, so I will tell you now: Where I am going, you cannot come" (v. 33).

In the light of His separation from His disciples, Jesus gave them a new commandment: "A new command I give you: Love one another. As I have loved you, so you must love one another. By this everyone will know that you are my disciples, if you love one another" (vv. 34–35).

The disciples did not concern themselves with the command of loving one another. As a matter of fact, they had been contending among themselves as to who would be the greatest (Luke 22:24). But they were very much interested in the fact that Jesus was leaving them. Simon Peter asked Jesus the question, "Lord, where are you going?" (John 13:36). Jesus replied, "Where I am going, you cannot follow now, but you will follow later" (v. 36). Peter persisted, however, and asked, "Lord, why can't I follow you now? I will lay down my life for you" (v. 37). Jesus answered Peter, "Will you really lay down your life for me? Very truly I tell you, before the rooster crows, you will disown me three times!" (v. 38). No doubt, Peter was sincere in his profession of loyalty to Jesus Christ, but he did not know how weak he was. The prophecy of Jesus that Peter would deny the Lord three times before the cock crowed was literally fulfilled the following morning.

JESUS AS THE VINE AND THE DISCIPLES AS THE BRANCHES

> I am the vine; you are the branches. If you remain
> in me and I in you, you will bear much fruit; apart
> from me you can do nothing. (John 15:5)

In John 15:1–8, Jesus opened His discussion of the disciples as those who would bear fruit for God. He declared, "I am the true vine" (v. 1). This is the seventh "I am" of Christ as recorded in the gospel of John. In John 6:35, Jesus said, "I am the bread of life." In John 8:12, Jesus revealed, "I am the light of the world." In John 10:7–9, Jesus stated, "I am the gate." In John 10:11–14, Jesus affirmed, "I am the good shepherd." In John 11:25, Jesus stated, "I am the resurrection and the life." In John 14:6, Jesus declared, "I am the way and the truth and the life."

In this final declaration, "I am the true vine," Jesus was comparing Himself to Israel as a vine that was planted but did not bear fruit (cf. Isa. 5:1–7). Enlarging on the figure, He declared, "My Father is the gardener. He cuts off every branch in me that bears no fruit, while every branch that does bear fruit he prunes so that it will be even more fruitful" (John 15:1–2).

When Jesus stated that the branches were in the vine, He was using a figure of speech. In John 14:20, He said, "You are in me." Believers since the day of Pentecost have been baptized and placed in God's plan of grace for those who put their trust in Christ. In John 15, however, where He spoke of being "in the vine," He was talking not about position but about fruitfulness. A branch appears superficially to be in the vine, but if there is no fruit, it is pruned. The gardener views it as only a superficial connection to the vine. Jesus was talking not about the security of a believer in Christ but rather about the state of fruitfulness that exists in a true believer yet does not exist in one who is merely a professing Christian.

To the disciples Jesus said, "You are already clean because of the word I have spoken to you" (John 15:3). In keeping with the illustration, the disciples cannot expect to bear fruit unless they remain in the vine, which would enable them to bear fruit. Jesus again affirmed that "I am the vine; you are the branches. If you remain in me and I in you, you will bear much fruit; apart from me you can do nothing" (v. 5). As in the case of a grapevine, however, some branches will not maintain a living connection with the vine and will be pruned. Accordingly, Jesus said, "If you do not remain in me, you are like a branch that is thrown away and withers; such branches are picked up, thrown into the fire and burned" (v. 6).

Various interpretations have arisen concerning this statement as expressing the idea that a person, once saved, can be lost. But Jesus contradicted such interpretation. In the gospel of John, Jesus affirmed that eternal life could not be lost (5:24). It is ultimately a question of what God does rather than what people do in contrast here to fruitfulness; it depends on what people do in relying on and drawing life from the vine. Jesus frequently talked in the gospel of John about the genuineness of salvation, which could not be lost (see also 1 Cor. 3:15; 9:27; 2 Cor. 5:10). The best explanation, however, is that it is referring to professing Christians who outwardly are joined to Christ but actually have no living connection and therefore cannot bear the fruit that can be expected of a fruitful branch. The branches do not become fruitful branches by bearing fruit; they become fruitful branches because of their abiding connection with the life of the vine.

If the disciples remained in vital relationship to Jesus Christ and depended on Him for fruitfulness, He promised, "If you remain in me and my words remain in you, ask whatever you wish, and it will done for you. This is to my Father's glory, that you bear much fruit, showing yourselves to be my disciples" (John 15:7–8). In the discourse on the vine, three degrees of fruitfulness are mentioned: bearing fruit (v. 2), being "more fruitful" (v. 2), and bearing "much fruit" (v. 8). One of the marks of a fruitful Christian is that he or she is in prayer fellowship with God and God can answer that person's prayers because they are to His glory.

THE WORLD WILL HATE TRUE DISCIPLES OF JESUS

> They have hated both me and my Father. But this is
> to fulfill what is written in their Law: "They hated
> me without reason." (John 15:24–25)

In John 15:18–25, Jesus revealed that just as the relationship of a disciple to the Father and to the Son was one of love, so, by contrast, the world would hate them because they also hated Christ. Jesus said:

> If the world hates you, keep in mind that it hated
> me first. If you belonged to the world, it would love

you as its own. As it is, you do not belong to the
world, but I have chosen you out of the world. That
is why the world hates you. Remember what I told
you: "A servant is not greater than his master." If
they persecuted me, they will persecute you also.
(vv. 18–20)

Jesus declared the world guilty because they rejected Him and
did not pay attention to His miracles (vv. 21–25).

THE COMING OF THE HOLY SPIRIT AS COUNSELOR

When the Advocate comes, whom I will send to
you from the Father—the Spirit of truth who goes
out from the Father—he will testify about me.
(John 15:26)

In John 15:26–27, Jesus gave His disciples a final word of
encouragement, similar to what He said in 14:26. Jesus assured His
disciples that the Spirit of truth would come and would testify to
them concerning Jesus (15:26). Just as the Spirit testified to them,
so they too must be a testimony for God because they had seen first-
hand His miracles and heard His public ministry (v. 27).

Taken as a whole, the Upper Room Discourse looks beyond the
death and resurrection of Christ and His ascension into heaven and
is a prediction concerning the moral and spiritual characteristics of
the world while Jesus is with the Father.

THE DISCIPLES TO EXPERIENCE PERSECUTION

> They will put you out of the synagogue; in fact, the time is coming when anyone who kills you will think they are offering a service to God. (John 16:2)

Having mentioned the disciples' coming persecution (John 15:18–20), Jesus in John 16:1–4 detailed some of their future experiences. The disciples would be put out of the synagogue, and those who killed them would think they were serving God (v. 2). The reason for this persecution was that those people did not know the Father or Jesus (v. 3). As Jesus would be absent from them, He told the disciples now so they would realize that prophecy was being fulfilled when it occurred.

THE COMING OF THE HOLY SPIRIT

> [Jesus] said to [the disciples]: "It is not for you to know the times or dates the Father has set by his own authority. But you will receive power when the Holy Spirit comes on you; and you will be my witnesses in Jerusalem, and in all Judea and Samaria, and to the ends of the earth." (Acts 1:7–8)

In many respects, the book of Acts, also written by Luke, is a continuation of Luke's gospel. In His post-resurrection ministry, Jesus instructed the disciples in Acts 1, "Do not leave Jerusalem, but wait for the gift my Father promised, which you have heard me speak about. For John baptized with water, but in a few days you will be baptized with the Holy Spirit" (vv. 4–5). The record of the fulfillment of this prophecy is given in Acts 2.

While Jesus was still with them, the disciples asked Him, "Lord, are you at this time going to restore the kingdom to Israel?" (1:6). It is most illuminating that at this point, after three and a half years of listening to Christ teach and going through the experiences of His death, resurrection, and post-resurrection ministry, the disciples were still not clear concerning the kingdom promises of the Old Testament. Jesus answered their question: "It is not for you to know the times or dates the Father has set by his own authority" (v. 7).

If they were incorrect in their expectation of literal fulfillment of the Old Testament promises of a kingdom on earth, this would have been a proper time to correct the disciples. The answer that Jesus gave, that it was not for them to know the time or the date—that is, the general time or the particular time—indicated the event was still ahead. God had not seen fit to reveal to them how these prophecies were to be fulfilled.

From the perspective of over two thousand years, it is obvious that God is fulfilling in this present age His purpose, unannounced in the Old Testament, of calling out a people from both Jews and Gentiles to form the church of Christ. It is also abundantly clear that the church does not fulfill the promises of the kingdom on earth as given to the people of Israel. As the book of Acts progresses, the disciples gradually realized that God was carrying out this program for Jew and Gentile first and, after this period, which is really a time of Gentile blessing, that He would resume His plan and purpose to fulfill the kingdom promise to Israel in connection with the second coming of Christ.

More important than the time of the kingdom, which God had not seen fit to reveal, Jesus told them of the coming of the Holy Spirit, which would be the main factor in the present dispensation. He said to them, "But you will receive power when the Holy Spirit comes on you; and you will be my witnesses in Jerusalem, and in all Judea and Samaria, and to the ends of the earth" (Acts 1:8). In subsequent events in the book of Acts, including Acts 2, the literal fulfillment of the promise was illustrated. All the Gospels agree that it was a duty of those left behind at the ascension to evangelize the world (Matt. 28:18–20; Mark 16:15–18; Luke 24:47–48; John 20:21–22).

7

DEFEATER OF DEATH: HOW JESUS'S DEATH AND RESURRECTION FULFILLED ANCIENT PROPHECIES

Incredibly, every detail of Jesus's life fulfilled prophecies concerning the Messiah. It should come as no surprise that His death would meet those same standards as well. The method and specifics of His death were largely outside His control, which made His fulfillment of those prophecies all the more amazing.

JESUS'S TRIUMPHAL ENTRY INTO JERUSALEM

> They took palm branches and went out to meet him. (John 12:13)

In John 12:12–19, we see the Lord coming to Jerusalem in an entry fit for a king. The tidings of Lazarus's resurrection and the accumulation of Jesus's ministry caused the crowds to welcome Him with palm branches (vv. 12–13). John recorded that the crowds shouted, "Hosanna! Blessed is he who comes in the name of the Lord! Blessed is the king of Israel!" (v. 13). In addition to quoting and fulfilling Zechariah 9:9, the crowd also quoted from Psalm 118:25–26.

John recorded that the disciples at the time did not recognize the significance of what they had seen and heard, but after Jesus's glorification, they realized that this occasion was a fulfillment of prophecy. John also added that the resurrection of Lazarus and this event of entering Jerusalem triumphantly served to spread the gospel so that many others believed in Jesus. This led the Pharisees to total exasperation, and they said, "See, this is getting us nowhere. Look how the whole world has gone after him!" (John 12:19).

THE WORLD HATED JESUS

> If the world hates you, keep in mind that it hated me first. (John 15:18)

In John 15:18–25, while Jesus had His followers, He was also ultimately led to the cross because of the fear, hatred, and persecution from those in authority. Just as the Psalms predicted (35:19; 69:4), many would be Jesus's enemies, who would hate Him without cause.

BETRAYED BY A FRIEND

> Jesus replied, "The one who has dipped his hand into the bowl with me will betray me." (Matt. 26:23)

Matthew 26:14–25 details Judas Iscariot's betrayal of Jesus. A Messianic psalm, Psalm 41, described a particular persecution: "Even my close friend, someone I trusted, one who shared my bread, has turned against me" (v. 9). This was fulfilled precisely by Judas, who had shared bread with Jesus many times. Jesus even called out His betrayer during the Passover, an important ritual of breaking bread together.

THIRTY PIECES OF SILVER

> Then one of the Twelve—the one called Judas Iscariot—went to the chief priests and asked, "What are you willing to give me if I deliver him over to you?" So they counted out for him thirty pieces of silver. (Matt. 26:14–15)

Matthew 26:14–16; 27:3–10 tells of the payment Judas received for his betrayal of Jesus. Not only did Scripture predict that a close friend would betray Jesus, but it even predicted the amount the traitor would be paid. Zechariah 11:12 prophesied that the forsaken Good Shepherd would be bought for "thirty pieces of silver." This was the same price Judas received for helping to hand over Jesus, the ultimate Good Shepherd.

JESUS'S ARREST AND BETRAYAL

> Jesus answered, "I told you that I am he. If you are looking for me, then let these men go." This

happened so that the words he had spoken would
be fulfilled: "I have not lost one of those you gave
me." (John 18:8–9)

In John 18:1–14, Jesus and His disciples had gone to a garden
across the brook Kidron, and there Judas and a detachment of
soldiers found Him. As they arrested Him, however, Jesus urged
them to let the disciples go (vv. 4–8). John added the comment,
"This happened so that the words he had spoken would be fulfilled:
'I have not lost one of those you gave me'" (v. 9; see also 6:39).
Peter, in his zeal to defend Christ, cut off the ear of the high priest's
servant. Jesus rebuked Peter, however, and healed and restored the
ear (Luke 22:49–51).

CONDEMNED BY FALSE WITNESSES

The chief priests and the whole Sanhedrin were
looking for false evidence against Jesus so that they
could put him to death. But they did not find any,
though many false witnesses came forward. (Matt.
26:59–60)

Matthew 26:59–61 connects to Psalm 27, yet another of David's
psalms in which he described persecution that would foreshadow the
trials of the Messiah. Just like David wrote, Jesus had "false witnesses
rise up against me, spouting malicious accusations" (v. 12).

JESUS'S ARREST AND PETER'S DENIAL AS FULFILLMENT OF SCRIPTURE

> Jesus answered, "You say that I am a king. In fact,
> the reason I was born and came into the world is to
> testify to the truth. Everyone on the side of truth
> listens to me." (John 18:37)

John's account of the trial and condemnation of Jesus leading up to His crucifixion (John 18:12–19:16) is not in itself prophecy but fulfilled predictions in both the Old Testament and the New Testament concerning the fact that Jesus would die.

THE PSALMIST'S LAMENT

> About three in the afternoon Jesus cried out in a
> loud voice, *"Eli, Eli, lema sabachthani?"* (which
> means "My God, my God, why have you forsaken
> me?"). (Matt. 27:46)

In Matthew 27:45–46, Jesus cried out from the cross, but He was not just exclaiming His pain. In fact, He was prophetically praying the words of the psalmist from Psalm 22:1: "My God, my God, why have you forsaken me?" When Jesus took the sins of the world on His shoulders, He actually became a sin offering and was rejected by God in the place of sinful humanity.

VINEGAR AND GALL FOR JESUS

> Immediately one of them ran and got a sponge.
> He filled it with wine vinegar, put it on a staff, and
> offered it to Jesus to drink. (Matt. 27:48)

Psalm 69:21 says, "They put gall in my food and gave me vinegar for my thirst." During Jesus's final moments of suffering, recorded in Matthew 27:47–49, the onlookers offered him vinegar in accordance with this prophecy.

HIS FRIENDS ABANDONED HIM

> Many women were there, watching from a distance.
> (Matt. 27:55)

Even though Jesus had accumulated a large group of dedicated followers, or "disciples," in his final moments of anguish, none of his devoted disciples dared stand by Him. Just as Psalm 38:11 predicted, "My friends and companions avoid me because of my wounds; my neighbors stay far away."

THE CRUCIFIXION OF JESUS

> Jesus said, "It is finished." With that, he bowed his
> head and gave up his spirit. (John 19:30)

In giving the details of the crucifixion of Christ in John 19:16–37, the apostle pointed out that there are several fulfillments of prophecy. One concerns the seamless garment of Christ, for which they cast lots as was predicted in Psalm 22:18: "They divided my clothes among them and cast lots for my garment" (John 19:24).

When Jesus declared, "I am thirsty" (v. 28), John also mentioned that Scripture had been fulfilled. He was referring to Psalm 69:21. Jesus, the One who could give the water of life (John 4:14; 7:38–39), here was suffering for the sins of the world. With His final statement, "It is finished" (19:30), Jesus indicated that He had completed the work of redemption and the price had been paid in full.

THE DEATH AND RESURRECTION OF CHRIST

> The soldiers therefore came and broke the legs of
> the first man who had been crucified with Jesus,
> and then those of the other. But when they came to
> Jesus and found that he was already dead, they did
> nor break his legs. (John 19:32–33)

John 19:31–42 details the preparation of Jesus's burial. The fact that Jesus's executioners did not break His legs (John 19:32–33) fulfilled the Scriptures: "Not one of his bones will be broken" (v. 36; cf. the predictions in Exod. 12:46; Num. 9:12; Ps. 34:20). John also quoted Scripture: "They will look on the one they have pierced" (John 19:37; see also Zech. 12:10).

The fact that Jesus was buried in the tomb of Joseph of Arimathea fulfilled the allusion in Isaiah 53:9, which indicated that He would be buried with the rich.

THREE DAYS OF RESURRECTION FULFILLED THE SIGN OF JONAH

> He then began to teach them that the Son of Man must suffer many things and be rejected by the elders, the chief priests and the teachers of the law, and that he must be killed and after three days rise again. (Mark 8:31)

In reply to some of the Pharisees and teachers of the law who demanded a miraculous sign, Jesus had replied that they would receive no sign except the sign of Jonah, for just as Jonah was in a huge fish three days and three nights, so Jesus would be in the heart of the earth three days and three nights. Nineveh, which repented at the message of Jonah, would rise up in judgment against them (Matt. 12:41). The Queen of the South would also condemn them because she honored Solomon, and now one greater than Solomon had appeared (v. 42). Jesus described the worthlessness of moral renewal without real faith as one of inviting evil spirits to take up their abode. Jesus stated, "That is how it will be with this wicked generation" (v. 45).

As the disciples on the road to Emmaus declared when Jesus appeared to them after His resurrection, it was "the third day since all this took place" (Luke 24:21).

THE RESURRECTION AS FULFILLMENT OF PROPHECY

> Do not hold on to me, for I have not yet ascended
> to the Father. Go instead to my brothers and tell
> them, "I am ascending to my Father and your
> Father, to my God and your God." (John 20:17)

In His resurrection, Christ fulfilled prophecies of the Old and New Testaments. Jesus revealed Himself first to Mary Magdalene (Mark 16:9–11; John 20:11–18); to the women returning a second time to the tomb (Matt. 28:8–10); to Peter (Luke 24:34; 1 Cor. 15:5); to the disciples on the road to Emmaus (Mark 16:12; Luke 24:30–32); to the disciples on the day of His resurrection in the evening, though Thomas was absent (Mark 16:14; Luke 24:36–43; John 20:19–25); and a week later to all the disciples, including Thomas (John 20:26–31; 1 Cor. 15:5).

Though the events of His resurrection were a fulfillment of prophecy, Jesus Himself did not introduce many new prophecies in John 20. In His conversation with Mary Magdalene, Jesus told her He was ascending to God the Father and it was not proper for her to hold Him to the earth. His ascension took place forty days later (Acts 1:3, 9–10).

In John 20:23, Jesus told the disciples, "If you forgive anyone's sins, their sins are forgiven; if you do not forgive them, they are not forgiven." The disciples had the power to acknowledge that sins were forgiven, but on the same basis as other Christians—that is, on the basis of the Word of God and its promises.

PETER AND THE HEALING OF THE LAME BEGGAR

> By faith in the name of Jesus, this man whom you
> see and know was made strong. It is Jesus' name
> and the faith that comes through him that has com-
> pletely healed him, as you can all see. (Acts 3:16)

In Acts 3:11–26, as the people looked expectantly on Peter and John because of the healing of the lame beggar, Peter delivered his sermonette, pointing out the background of Jesus and His being crucified (vv. 13–15). Peter announced that this lame beggar had been healed by faith in Jesus (v. 16). He further informed them that though they had acted in ignorance in rejecting Jesus, what they had done fulfilled the prophecies of the Old Testament indicating Christ would suffer (vv. 17–18).

On the basis of this, Peter exhorted them:

> Repent, then, and turn to God, so that your sins
> may be wiped out, that times of refreshing may
> come from the Lord, and that he may send the
> Messiah, who has been appointed for you—even
> Jesus. Heaven must receive him until the time
> comes for God to restore everything, as he prom-
> ised long ago through his holy prophets. For Moses
> said, "The Lord your God will raise up for you a
> prophet like me from among your own people; you
> must listen to everything he tells you. Anyone who

does not listen to him will be completely cut off from their people."

Indeed, beginning with Samuel, all the prophets who have spoken have foretold these days. And you are heirs of the prophets and of the covenant God made with your fathers. He said to Abraham, "Through your offspring all peoples on earth will be blessed." When God raised up his servant, he sent him first to you to bless you by turning each of you from your wicked ways. (vv. 19–26)

Peter gave the certain prediction that Jesus is now in heaven and that the time of restoration promised Israel through the holy prophecies is still in the future, pending His return.

CHRIST'S DEATH FULFILLED ISAIAH

The eunuch asked Philip, "Tell me, please, who is the prophet [Isaiah] talking about, himself or someone else?" Then Philip began with that very passage of Scripture and told him the good news about Jesus. (Acts 8:34–35)

In Acts 8:26–40, an Ethiopian eunuch was reading the words of Isaiah and came upon a very confusing passage. It described the coming Messiah in this way: "He was led like a lamb to the slaughter, and as a sheep before its shearer is silent, so he did not open his mouth. By oppression and judgment he was taken away. Yet who of his generation protested? For he was cut off from the land of the living" (Isa. 53:7–8). One of Jesus's followers, a deacon named Philip, was able to explain to the eunuch how Jesus's very specific form of death had fulfilled Old Testament prophecy.

CHRIST'S DEATH BROUGHT FORGIVENESS OF SINS

> All the prophets testify about him that everyone who believes in him receives forgiveness of sins through his name. (Acts 10:43)

In Acts 10, Peter preached to Cornelius that Jesus Christ's death actually earned forgiveness of sins for fallen humanity. This was not a new or radical teaching but had been predicted by Isaiah many years before. "Yet it was the LORD's will to crush him and cause him to suffer, and ... the LORD makes his life an offering for sin" (Isa. 53:10).

Paul then furthered this point in Acts 13:38–39: "Therefore, my friends, I want you to know that through Jesus the forgiveness of sins is proclaimed to you. Through him everyone who believes is set free from every sin, a justification you were not able to obtain under the law of Moses."

CHRIST IS THE FOUNDATION OF RELATIONSHIP WITH THE FATHER

> You are no longer foreigners and strangers, but fellow citizens with God's people and also members of his

household, built on the foundation of the apostles
and prophets, with Christ Jesus himself as the chief
cornerstone. (Eph. 2:19–20)

Isaiah 28:16 predicted that the Messiah would be a "cornerstone," and both Ephesians 2:19–22 and 1 Peter 2:6 recognize Jesus
as that cornerstone upon which all of us build our faith.

CHRIST'S INNOCENCE FULFILLED ISAIAH

He committed no sin,
and no deceit was found in his mouth.
(1 Pet. 2:22)

Christ's death was truly a wrongful execution, as stated in 1 Peter
2:21–25. Not only was Jesus innocent of a crime, He was the only
human being who has ever lived an entirely sinless life. The words of
Isaiah (53:4–6, 9) anticipated this unique aspect of the Messiah and
His death.

CHRIST'S LIFE OF PERFECT OBEDIENCE

You have made him a little lower than the angels;
You have crowned him with glory and honor,
And set him over the works of Your hands.
You have put all things in subjection under his
feet. (Heb. 2:7–8 NKJV)

The author of Hebrews focused extensively on connecting Christ's death with Old Testament religion and understanding. This is seen most concisely in two sections of the book of Hebrews, in chapters 2 and 10 (esp., 2:6–8; 10:1–14). In chapter 2, Hebrews shows how the Messiah was above creation and then was brought down to the level of mankind. This was predicted in Psalm 8:5: "You have made him a little lower than the angels" (NKJV).

In addition, Hebrews 10 shows how Christ's death on the cross fulfilled Psalm 40. As the psalm states, these verses refer to David's praise to the Lord and his desire to do the will of God. This, however, also anticipated prophetically Christ's perfect obedience and His sacrifice as superior to the sacrifices of the Mosaic law. The argument of Hebrews 10 is that Christ in His perfect sacrifice supplied that which the law could not do with its temporary sacrifices. Key words in the psalm are "righteousness," "faithfulness," "salvation," "lovingkindness," and "truth" (vv. 9–10 NKJV).

8

PROMISED SALVATION: JESUS'S PROPHECIES OF ETERNAL REWARDS FOR HIS FOLLOWERS

By now, we have seen example after example of the Father's love and care for His children. Each prophecy fulfilled is confirmation that He is sovereign, powerful, and mighty to save. Thankfully, His provision isn't limited to our time here on earth; Jesus consistently proclaimed that those who believed in Him would have eternal life. Here are many examples of Jesus's prophecies of salvation for His followers.

THE REWARDS OF HIS DISCIPLES

> "Truly I tell you," Jesus replied, "no one who has left home or brothers or sisters or mother or father or children or fields for me and the gospel will fail to receive a hundred times as much in this present age ... and in the age to come eternal life." (Mark 10:29–30)

As we see in Mark 10:28–31 and Luke 18:28–30, even Jesus's closest followers struggled with understanding the promises of salvation. After all, they had given up friends, family, and livelihoods to wander penniless with their rabbi. They would suffer persecution and death. It is understandable, then, that the disciples at one point "called the question."

In regard to the disciples' question as to what they would receive in eternity, Jesus replied, "No one who has left home or brothers or sisters or mother or father or children or fields for me and the gospel will fail to receive a hundred times as much in this present age: homes, brothers, sisters, mothers, children and fields—along with persecution—and in the age to come eternal life. But many who are first will be last, and the last first" (Mark 10:29–31). In making these promises, Jesus was asserting that not only are there some rewards that are present for a believer and follower of Christ but that also other rewards will be given abundantly in heaven.

JESUS PROMISES ETERNAL LIFE

> Whoever believes in the Son has eternal life, but whoever rejects the Son will not see life, for God's wrath remains on them. (John 3:36)

In John 3, when Jesus testified to Nicodemus concerning the difficulty of accepting spiritual truth, He stated, "Just as Moses lifted up the snake in the wilderness, so the Son of Man must be lifted up, that everyone who believes may have eternal life in him. For God so loved the world that he gave his one and only Son, that whoever believes in him shall not perish but have eternal life" (vv. 14–16).

In alluding to Moses's lifting up the snake in the wilderness, Jesus was referring to Numbers 21:6–9. When the children of Israel complained about not having food and water to their liking, Numbers recorded that God sent venomous snakes among the people and caused many to die (v. 6). When the people of Israel confessed that they had sinned, the Lord instructed Moses to make a bronze snake and place it on a pole, and if the people were bitten by the snakes, they could look at the bronze snake and be healed (vv. 8–9).

Using this historical illustration, Jesus declared that He also "must be lifted up" (John 3:14). Just as in the case of Israel when they looked at the bronze serpent in faith and were healed, so Jesus predicted that when they looked at Him lifted up, they would believe and have eternal life (v. 15). In referring to being lifted up, Jesus was referring to His crucifixion and the need for them to go to the cross in faith in order to have salvation through Him. Jesus concluded this with the great affirmation that the gift of God's Son was an act of love and that "whoever believes in him shall not perish but have eternal life" (v. 16). No doubt, the disciples did not understand what Jesus was referring to until after His death and resurrection.

As a summary of this important chapter, the apostle John declared, "Whoever believes in the Son has eternal life, but whoever rejects the Son will not see life, for God's wrath remains on them" (v. 36). This verse provides a marvelous prophecy that belief in Jesus as the Son assures an individual of eternal life in contrast to those who reject Jesus, who not only forfeit life but also are under God's wrath.

JESUS'S TESTIMONY TO THE SAMARITAN WOMAN

> Jesus answered, "Everyone who drinks this water
> will be thirsty again, but whoever drinks the water I
> give them will never thirst. Indeed, the water I give
> them will become in them a spring of water welling
> up to eternal life." (John 4:13–14)

The journey between Judea and Galilee required going through Samaria, the direct route that Jesus and His disciples used, or to go around by the east through Perea. We see in John 4 that after journeying all day, Jesus and His disciples came as far as Jacob's well located in Samaria. The disciples went into the village to buy food. As Jesus sat by the well, a Samaritan woman came to draw water. Jesus, fully aware of her spiritual need, asked her for a drink (v. 7).

The Samaritan woman, well aware of the antagonism between Samaritans and Jews, was surprised that He would have anything to do with her. When she questioned why Jesus was willing to ask for the drink, Jesus answered her: "If you knew the gift of God and who it is that asks you for a drink, you would have asked him and he would have given you living water" (v. 10). The Samaritan woman replied, of course, that Jesus had nothing with which to draw water, and after all, His forefathers—Jacob and his sons—had drawn water from the well. Naturally, it raised the question as to how He could give her living water (vv. 11–12).

Jesus then pointed out that worship is not a matter of place but a matter of true worship in spirit and in truth (v. 23). The Samaritan woman replied, "'I know that Messiah' (called Christ) 'is coming. When he comes, he will explain everything to us'" (v. 25). Jesus then declared to her, "I, the one speaking to you—I am he" (v. 26).

At this point in the narrative, the disciples had returned and were surprised that Jesus would talk to a Samaritan woman but, nevertheless, did not ask Him why. When they urged Jesus to eat, He replied, "I have food to eat that you know nothing about" (v. 32). When the disciples could not understand this, He told them, "My food ... is to do the will of him who sent me and to finish his work" (v. 34). Jesus then pointed out to them that the fields were white unto harvest—speaking, of course, of a spiritual harvest.

When the woman testified to the inhabitants of her village that Jesus had told her all she had ever done, because of her sinful life they naturally came out of curiosity to see One who knew all about her, and many believed (vv. 39–41). The gospel of John, designed to lead people to faith in Christ that they may receive eternal life, has now added the Samaritan woman as a possible candidate for salvation along with Nicodemus, a law-abiding Jew. In the process of leading the Samaritan woman to faith in Him, Jesus had demonstrated His omniscience and His capacity to give eternal life.

JESUS'S CLAIM OF EQUALITY WITH THE FATHER

> For just as the Father raises the dead and gives them life, even so the Son gives life to whom he is pleased to give it. (John 5:21)

Because Jesus had healed the invalid at the pool of Bethesda on the Sabbath, the Jews persecuted Him (John 5:2–16). Because Jesus claimed God as His Father, the Jews persecuted Him all the more because they regarded this as a statement that He was equal to the Father (vv. 17–18).

In His exposition on His union with the Father, He declared that the Father loves Him (v. 20), that He has the power to raise the dead even as the Father does (v. 21), and that the Father has entrusted all judgment to the Son (vv. 22–23). Accordingly, those who do not honor the Son do not honor the Father (v. 23).

This led Jesus to declare, "Very truly I tell you, whoever hears my word and believes him who sent me has eternal life and will not be judged but has crossed over from death to life" (v. 24).

Expanding further on His ability to save, Jesus said,

> Very truly I tell you, a time is coming and has now come when the dead will hear the voice of the Son of God and those who hear will live. For as the Father has life in himself, so he has granted the Son also to have life in himself. And he has given him authority to judge because he is the Son of Man.
>
> Do not be amazed at this, for a time is coming when all who are in their graves will hear his voice and come out—those who have done what is good will rise to live, and those who have done what is evil will rise to be condemned. (vv. 25–29)

The broad prophecies revealed by the Savior here predict, first of all, the salvation of individuals who hear the facts about Christ and, as a result of believing, will live eternally. Just as Jesus has life in Himself from the Father, so He has authority to judge as the Son of Man (v. 26). For further confirmation of Christ's ability, Jesus called attention to the fact that those in the grave, referring to those who have died physically, will someday hear His voice and come out of the grave, with the result that they will be judged concerning their life on earth, whether good or bad (vv. 28–29). In asserting this fact of judgment, Christ Jesus was not teaching that all the resurrections will occur at the same time, as other Scriptures make clear that there will be a series of resurrections and the wicked will not be judged until all the righteous are raised.

In these predictions and assertions, the apostle John recorded one fact after another supporting his belief that Jesus is the Son of God and the only Savior who can give eternal life.

JESUS'S DEITY AND HIS POWER TO GIVE ETERNAL LIFE

> My sheep listen to my voice; I know them, and they follow me. I give them eternal life, and they shall never perish; no one will snatch them out of my hand. (John 10:27–28)

John 10 shows how the sayings of Jesus divided His audience. Some claimed that He was demon possessed, but others claimed that, nevertheless, His miracles demonstrated that He was a genuine prophet (vv. 19–21).

When the Jews addressed Him, "How long will you keep us in suspense? If you are the Messiah, tell us plainly" (v. 24), Jesus replied that He had given them adequate proof. His miracles testified to His claim to be genuine (v. 25). The reason they were having trouble believing Him was that they were not His sheep (v. 26). Jesus declared, "My sheep listen to my voice; I know them, and they follow me. I give them eternal life, and they shall never perish; no one will snatch them out of my hand" (vv. 27–28).

This passage is another assertion that those who are born again have received an eternal salvation in the eternal life that they receive. Jesus promised that they would never perish or fall from their exalted position. He said, "No one will snatch them out of my hand. My Father, who has given them to me, is greater than all; no one can snatch them out of my Father's hand. I and the Father are one" (vv. 28–30).

As a double assurance of the certainty of their salvation, Jesus declared that they are not only in His hands but also in the Father's hands, and no one can take them out of the Father's hands. When He concluded with the statement "I and the Father are one" (v. 30), the Jews recognized this as a claim to deity and picked up stones to stone Him (v. 31). Jesus asked them why they were offended. They replied, "We are not stoning you for any good work ... but for blasphemy, because you, a mere man, claim to be God" (v. 33).

LAZARUS AND JESUS: TWO STORIES OF DEATH CONQUERED

> I am the resurrection and the life. The one who believes in me will live, even though they die; and whoever lives by believing in me will never die. (John 11:25–26)

Covering the death and resurrection of Lazarus, John 11 is an appropriate introduction of the death and resurrection of Christ, which occurred not many days later. It centers in the great truth that in Jesus there is resurrection and life.

When Jesus heard of Lazarus's illness, He declared, "This sickness will not end in death. No, it is for God's glory so that God's Son may be glorified through it" (v. 4).

For His own reasons, Jesus intentionally delayed His return so that Lazarus had been dead several days before He arrived. Martha, who went out to greet Him, said as no doubt they had said many times in His absence, "Lord ... if you had been here, my brother would not have died. But I know that even now God will give you whatever you ask" (vv. 21–22). Though she did not expect Jesus to raise Lazarus, she did assert that He had the power to do it.

This gave Jesus occasion to discuss resurrection with her, and Jesus said to Martha, "Your brother will rise again" (v. 23). Martha in her reply asserted her faith that all would be resurrected eventually. Jesus went on to affirm more than the hope of all for resurrection, and He said to Martha, "I am the resurrection and the life. The one who believes in me will live, even though they die; and whoever lives by believing in me will never die. Do you believe this?" (vv. 25–26). Martha in reply came back to the basic fact that she believed Jesus was the Christ, the Son of God (v. 27).

When Jesus arrived at Lazarus's tomb, He performed perhaps His most impressive miracle. Jesus prayed to God the Father: "Father, I thank you that you have heard me. I knew that you always hear me, but I said this for the benefit of the people standing here, that they may believe that you sent me" (vv. 41–42).

Then Jesus, speaking with a loud vice, said, "Lazarus, come out!" (v. 43). To the astonishment of those who observed, Lazarus came out of the tomb in his grave clothes. Jesus ordered them to take the grave clothes from him and let him go (v. 44).

The obvious great miracle that occurred influenced many others to put their trust in Jesus (v. 45), but the chief priests and the Pharisees were upset by this demonstration of the power of God, and they said, "Here is this man performing many signs. If we let him go on like this, everyone will believe in him, and then the Romans will come and take away both our temple and our nation" (vv. 47–48).

The utter blindness of the Pharisees to the significance of what had happened at the tomb of Lazarus and their selfish desire to maintain their own place of leadership are a constant reminder of the blindness of the human heart untouched by the grace of God when faced with the facts of Jesus Christ.

JESUS'S REVELATION OF GOD'S PROVISION FOR HIS TROUBLED DISCIPLES

My Father's house has many rooms; if that were not so, would I have told you that I am going there to prepare a place for you? And if I go and prepare a place for you, I will come back and take you to be with me that you also may be where I am. (John 14:2–3)

In John 14, the disciples were deeply troubled. They had heard Jesus announce that one was going to betray Him. They had heard Him tell Peter that he was going to deny Him three times. Most of all, they were concerned about the fact that Jesus said He was going to leave them and they could not follow (13:36). At this point in their last night together, Jesus prophetically outlined God's provisions for them as troubled disciples in a troubled world.

Jesus, first of all, exhorted them not to be troubled, but He said that instead they should "believe in God; believe also in me" (14:1). This command can be literally translated, "Keep on trusting in God; keep on trusting in me." The secret of the untroubled heart in a troubled world is complete trust in God. In exhorting them to do this, He was giving the whole answer. Recognizing, however, that all of us, including the disciples, are weak, the rest of the chapter outlines the support basis for this trust in God.

In light of His departure, Jesus promised them that He would return: "My Father's house has many rooms; if that were not so, would I have told you that I am going there to prepare a place for you? And if I go and prepare a place for you, I will come back and take you to be with me that you also may be where I am" (vv. 2–3).

This was an entirely new revelation to be contrasted to Christ's earlier revelation concerning His second coming to judge the world. This was a coming with an entirely different context, and its purpose was to take them out of the world and take them to the Father's house, which clearly refers to heaven, where Jesus has gone before to prepare a place for those who believe in Him. This is the first reference in the New Testament to what Paul later referred to as the rapture of the church (1 Cor. 15:51–58; 1 Thess. 4:13–18).

The disciples were unprepared emotionally and theologically to receive this truth, which John recorded many years later in this gospel. They did comprehend, however, that Jesus was going to leave them. This was a devastating truth to them because they had been with Christ for three and a half years and had left their homes and their occupations in order to be His disciples. They simply did not understand what Jesus meant when He said He was going to leave them. Scripture records that Jesus had closed His remarks by saying, "You know the way to the place where I am going" (John 14:4).

Thomas, as he contemplated this sentence, did not know where Jesus was going, and the other disciples probably had the same problem. Thomas said to Jesus, "Lord, we don't know where you are going, so how can we know the way?" (v. 5). This was a logical statement because if people do not know their destination, they do not know where they are going. This is a profound truth that affects all of our lives. Knowing our ultimate destination is a part of God's program of reassuring troubled disciples. On the other hand, Jesus was referring to heaven, and certainly Thomas and the other disciples should have known that this was their ultimate destination.

Jesus's answer to Thomas was both profound and simple: "I am the way and the truth and the life. No one comes to the Father except through me" (v. 6). There are few statements in any language or any book that can rival this for profound truth.

Jesus is the way or the road to heaven; this truth is not accepted by the world but is the mainstay of Christians who put their trust in God.

Jesus also said, "I am … the truth." All things are true because of God's laws and revelation, and Jesus is the source of this order in the universe. All truth is true only as it is related in some way to Jesus Christ as the truth.

Jesus also declared, "I am … the life." Again we see the profound truth that only in Jesus are eternal life and blessing in the life to come possible. All the philosophies of the world and the schemes of mankind have never been able to substitute anything for God's plan of Jesus as the way to heaven as the ultimate test of truth and the ultimate bestower of eternal life.

In addition to the great truth that Christ Himself was going to indwell believers, an additional dispensational truth characteristic of the present age from Pentecost was predicted in John 14:20: "On that day you will realize that I am in my Father, and you are in me, and I am in you." The expression "I am in you" refers to Christ's indwelling, but "you are in me" presents a truth foreign to the Old Testament but realized by Christians baptized into Christ. The gracious provision of God is not only that God is in us but also that we are vitally related to Jesus Christ and share the same eternal life. It is not too much to say that verse 20 is one of the great revelations of the New Testament and characterizes the present age as a distinct dispensation.

Once again, Jesus referred to the need to obey His commands and to love Him. He promised, "The one who loves me will be loved by my Father, and I too will love them and show myself to them" (v. 21). The disciples did not show too much interest in the fact of the love of Christ or being loved by the Father, but Judas (not Iscariot) asked the question, "But, Lord, why do you intend to show yourself to us and not to the world?" (v. 22). Jesus replied that a new relationship existed between Him and the disciples as well as the Father and the disciples. He said, "Anyone who loves me will obey my teaching. My Father will love them, and we will come to them and make our home with them" (v. 23). Here was an additional fact: Not only would Jesus and the Holy Spirit indwell a believer but also

God the Father would make the believer's body His home. Those who do not love Jesus and obey Him know nothing of this marvelous truth (v. 24).

The final work of God on behalf of the troubled disciples was His marvelous peace: "Peace I leave with you; my peace I give you. I do not give to you as the world gives. Do not let your hearts be troubled and do not be afraid" (v. 27). This remarkable statement came from Jesus, who knew that in the next twenty-four hours He would die the awful death of crucifixion and His body would be in the tomb. What did Jesus mean by "my peace"? The peace that Christ was referring to goes beyond the prophecy of death and resurrection of Christ and beyond ascension to the ultimate disposal and judgment of all things.

Jesus knew that in the end God would triumph and that His death on the cross would be rewarded by the heritage of millions of souls being saved. He also knew that though the disciples were troubled, their troubles were temporary and their ultimate peace was to be realized. The peace that Christ gives is more than a psychological peace, more than an act of human will, and one of the marvelous things that comes when disciples of Jesus who put their faith in God realize the tremendous assets and provisions God has made for them as Christians. Because of this, it is possible to be at peace even though disciples may live in a troubled world.

Jesus again referred to His departure and said that He was predicting it in advance and that they would know it was of God for Him to go to the Father and to come back (vv. 28–29). He told them that after He departed, "the prince of this world is coming. He has no hold over me, but he comes so that the world may learn that

I love the Father and do exactly what my Father has commanded me" (vv. 30–31). The "prince of this world" is a reference to Satan, and Jesus was, of course, alluding to the continued activity of Satan during the period that He was going back to the Father. The ultimate triumph over Satan, however, was assured. At this point in their evening together, they left the upper room and proceeded toward the garden of Gethsemane.

BELIEVERS AS HEIRS INHERITING GLORY

> I consider that our present sufferings are not worth comparing with the glory that will be revealed in us. For the creation waits in eager expectation for the children of God to be revealed. (Rom. 8:18–19)

In Romans 8, the true believer in Christ is described as having no condemnation (v. 1) and as one who is living under the control of the Holy Spirit. Even though this does not produce a perfect moral life, it nevertheless characterizes the believer who is living under the new nature rather than the old (v. 13). Present experience of salvation is the forerunner of that which is prophesied. If the believer is now a child of God, then that believer is also the heir of God (v. 17). As such, we may share some sufferings in this present life, but we also will share in the glory to come.

Contrasting our present suffering with future glory helps a Christian to realize what Paul stated: "I consider that our present sufferings are not worth comparing with the glory that will be revealed in us" (v. 18). The sufferings of a Christian are paralleled by sufferings in the world as a whole, for all creation is groaning and suffering like a woman giving birth (vv. 22–23). When Christians experience suffering, they all the more anticipate the full meaning of being adopted as children of God. Though this takes place in our present lives, when God recognizes Christians as His children, it gives a basis for hope that ultimately the sufferings will cease and makes it possible to hope patiently (v. 25). Even though some Christians may not know how to pray under certain circumstances, the promise is given that the Holy Spirit will pray as their intercessor (vv. 26–27).

Having been saved, Christians enter into the divine process of ultimate glorification described by Paul: "For those God foreknew he also predestined to be conformed to the image of his Son, that he might be the firstborn among many brothers and sisters. And those he predestined, he also called; those he called, he also justified; those he justified, he also glorified" (vv. 29–30).

On the basis of God's sovereign work for believers, which will not be consummated until they are presented perfect in glory, Paul stated the great truth that Christians can "know that in all things God works for the good of those who love him, who have been called according to his purpose" (v. 28). The point is that Christians were predestined before they were saved, and they were called and justified when they were saved. Now being justified and declared righteous by God, their next state will be one of glorification.

All of this, of course, is based on grace because Christians have been chosen, and their salvation has been possible because God did not spare His own Son (v. 32). There is no danger of Christians ever coming into condemnation and being declared lost. This is because they are seen in Christ, who died and was resurrected and is supported by His present intercession in heaven: "Christ Jesus who died—more than that, who was raised to life—is at the right hand of God and is also interceding for us" (v. 34).

The complete safety of the believer is presented in the classic conclusion of this chapter, in which Paul declared that nothing can separate a Christian from the love of Christ (v. 35). While it is true that Christians may face death and suffering as martyrs, it is also true that Christians conquer through Christ who loves them.

Paul declared his own faith and the content of every Christian's faith: "For I am convinced that neither death nor life, neither angels nor demons, neither the present nor the future, nor any powers, neither height nor depth, nor anything else in all creation, will be able to separate us from the love of God that is in Christ Jesus our Lord" (vv. 38–39). This detailed summary covers the whole gospel experience of mankind. Like all other aspects of our salvation, it is based on grace rather than reward. But having entered by faith into the grace that is in Christ Jesus, the believer has the certain hope that what is promised will certainly be fulfilled.

THE NECESSITY OF CHRIST'S RESURRECTION

> For if the dead are not raised, then Christ has not been raised either. And if Christ has not been raised, your faith is futile; you are still in your sins. Then those also who have fallen asleep in Christ are lost. If only for this life we have hope in Christ, we are of all people most to be pitied. (1 Cor. 15:16–19)

After offering proof of the resurrection of Christ, 1 Corinthians 15 then states that the resurrection of Christ is important because apart from this there would be a question as to whether Jesus was who He claimed to be: the Son of God, who had the power to lay down His life and take it again (vv. 3–8, 12–19; John 10:17–18). Accordingly, Paul said, "And if Christ has not been raised, our preaching is useless and so is your faith" (1 Cor. 15:14). Again, he stated, "And if Christ has not been raised, your faith is futile; you are still in your sins" (v. 17). The fact of resurrection makes our hope extend into eternity, not to this life only (v. 19).

THE ORDER OF THE RESURRECTIONS

> For as in Adam all die, so in Christ all will be made
> alive. (1 Cor. 15:22)

In 1 Corinthians 15:20–28, we are reminded how history records that Jesus died and rose again. As such, He is "the firstfruits of those who have fallen asleep" (v. 20). Though others have been restored to life in both the Old Testament and the New Testament, it may be assumed that they died again and returned to the grave. A new order began in Christ with Him receiving the body that will last for eternity. Because He has received a resurrection body, those who are raised after Him may receive a similar body and will not die again. Tabitha (or Dorcas), however, was merely restored to this life (Acts 9:36–42). It was proper for Christ to die and be resurrected first and then for others in their proper order to be resurrected (1 Cor. 15:22–23).

When human history has run its course and the millennial kingdom has been fulfilled, the final judgment on the wicked (Rev. 20:11–15) will take place, when Christ will be able to present the conquered world to God the Father. "Then the end will come, when he hands over the kingdom to God the Father after he has destroyed all dominion, authority and power" (1 Cor. 15:24). In some sense, God's kingdom will continue forever as God necessarily directs His entire rule over creation.

THE NATURE OF THE RESURRECTED BODY

> So will it be with the resurrection of the dead. The
> body that is sown is perishable, it is raised imperish-
> able; it is sown in dishonor, it is raised in glory; it
> is sown in weakness, it is raised in power; it is sown
> a natural body, it is raised a spiritual body. (1 Cor.
> 15:42–44)

In 1 Corinthians 15:35–50, the question is raised concerning what kind of body will be received in resurrection. Paul used the analogy of planting seed. Obviously, the body that will be resurrected is like the seed that is planted, but the seed itself perishes. Even in the natural world, people have bodies that are different from the bodies of animals or birds (v. 39). The inanimate bodies in space, such as the sun, the moon, and the stars, likewise, have different qualities (vv. 40–41).

The resurrection body, therefore, will have resemblance to the body that is sown or buried but will be raised with different qualities:

"It is sown a natural body, it is raised a spiritual body" (v. 44). In our natural world, the natural body comes first, then later the body that is spiritual, or suited for heaven (vv. 45–46).

In resurrection, human beings will be given another human body and, especially in the case of the saved, will have a body that is rendered imperishable, holy, and suited for the service and worship of God. As Paul concluded, it is impossible for those in their natural bodies to go into eternity unchanged. That which is perishable must become imperishable (v. 50).

THE MYSTERY OF THE RESURRECTION OF THE CHURCH

> For the trumpet will sound, the dead will be raised imperishable, and we will be changed. (1 Cor. 15:52)

Looking to 1 Corinthians 15:51–58, we see that although the normal order for all humans is to live, die, and then be subject to resurrection, there will be one grand exception at the end of the age. In history, Elijah and Enoch were caught up to heaven without dying (2 Kings 2:11; Heb. 11:5). At the rapture of the church, however, a whole generation of those who are saved will be caught up to heaven without dying. This will constitute the grand exception to the normal rule of death and resurrection.

This translation without dying was revealed by Paul: "Listen, I tell you a mystery: We will not all sleep, but we will all be changed—in a flash, in the twinkling of an eye, at the last trumpet. For the trumpet will sound, the dead will be raised imperishable, and we will be changed. For the perishable must clothe itself with the imperishable, and the mortal with immortality" (1 Cor. 15:51–53).

What can be known about the resurrection body? Much can be learned about our resurrection body by studying the resurrection body of Jesus Christ. From these scriptures and 1 Corinthians 15, it is obvious that those raised from the dead will share the rapture with those who are living on earth at the time of the rapture. Those who are raised and those who are translated will resemble what they were in earthly life. Jesus Christ was recognized, and though He had a new resurrection body, it still bore similarity to the body before the crucifixion.

Not only will living Christians be caught up to heaven without dying, but those Christians who have died also will be resurrected. Both will receive their new bodies that are suited for heaven. As Paul stated, they will be imperishable and will never be subject to decay, and they will be immortal, not subject to death (1 Cor. 15:53). They will also be free from sin and be the objects of God's grace and blessing throughout eternity.

At the rapture of the church, there will be a victory over death and the grave. Paul wrote, "Death has been swallowed up in victory. 'Where, O death, is your victory? Where, O death, is your sting?'" (vv. 54–55). He was quoting Isaiah 25:8, which states that God will "swallow up death forever," and Hosea 13:14, in which God said, "I will deliver this people from the power of the grave; I will redeem them from death. Where, O death, are your plagues? Where, O grave, is your destruction?" This doctrine is stated with greater clarity in the New Testament as Paul traced the victory through Jesus

Christ: "But thanks be to God! He gives us the victory through our Lord Jesus Christ" (1 Cor. 15:57).

In light of the great doctrine of the resurrection and translation and the imminent hope of the Lord's return, believers are exhorted to make the most of their remaining time on earth. Paul wrote, "Therefore, my dear brothers and sisters, stand firm. Let nothing move you. Always give yourselves fully to the work of the Lord, because you know that your labor in the Lord is not in vain" (v. 58).

Believers should stand firm because they are standing on the rock Christ Jesus and on the sure promises of God. They should not allow the vicissitudes of life and the sorrows and burdens that come to move them away from confidence in God. While living out their lives on earth, they are to engage in the work of the Lord, because they know that following this life at the judgment seat of Christ they will be rewarded and their "labor in the Lord is not in vain" (v. 58). This passage dealing with the rapture of the church coupled with Paul's earlier revelation in 1 Thessalonians 4:14–17 constitute the principal passages on this great truth of the Lord's coming and the bright hope that it could be soon.

9

CHRIST'S ENCORE: HOW JESUS WILL COME BACK AT THE SECOND COMING

Jesus spoke extensively about His return. He consistently proclaimed that His time on earth would not be His last. After His death and resurrection, He would come again, bringing the completeness of the kingdom of God with Him.

THE END OF THE AGE

> Then will appear the sign of the Son of Man in heaven. And then all the peoples of the earth will mourn when they will see the Son of Man coming on the clouds of heaven, with power and great glory. (Matt. 24:30)

The prophecies of Christ in His sermon on the Mount of Olives were delivered to four of the disciples: Peter, James, John, and Andrew (Mark 13:3). His discourse was in response to the disciples' questioning: "Tell us, when will these things happen? And what will be the sign that they are all about to be fulfilled?" (v. 4). They had reference to the previous prediction of Christ that the magnificent temple would be destroyed, which did not fit the disciples' expectation of the coming kingdom.

It is evident that the gospels of Matthew, Mark, and Luke recorded only a portion of this discourse, and the full picture is given by putting together the revelation in each of the three gospels. This should be understood in light of the fact that Jesus had declared the moral principles of the kingdom in the Sermon on the Mount (Matt. 5–7) and had described the present age (Matt. 13).

In Matthew 24–25 (see also Mark 13:1–27; Luke 21:5–36), Jesus described the period following His death and resurrection and ascension and extending to the end of the tribulation period of His second coming. The disciples were still having a great deal of difficulty understanding how this fit in with their messianic expectations.

SIGNS OF HIS SECOND COMING

> Watch out that no one deceives you. For many will come in my name, claiming, "I am the Messiah," and will deceive many. You will hear of wars and rumors of wars, but see to it that you are not alarmed. Such things must happen, but the end is still to come (Matt. 24:4–6)

In Matthew 24:1–14 (see also Mark 13:5–13; Luke 21:5–19), Christ delivered a sharp rebuke against the Pharisees and Sadducees for their hypocrisy and unbelief. This had come to a conclusion when Jesus lamented over Jerusalem for its long history of rejecting the prophets and killing those sent to them with the truth. He pronounced a solemn curse on Jerusalem, saying, "Look, your house is left to you desolate. For I tell you, you will not see me again until you say, 'Blessed is he who comes in the name of the Lord'" (Matt. 23:38–39).

A little later, after Jesus had left the temple, the disciples called His attention to the magnificence of the temple (24:1). Jesus came back, however, with a devastating prophecy: "Truly I tell you, not one stone here will be left on another; every one will be thrown down" (v. 2).

This prophecy alarmed the disciples. Four of them, Peter, Andrew, James, and John, asked in a private meeting with Jesus, "When will this happen, and what will be the sign of your coming and of the end of the age?" (v. 3; Mark 13:3–4; Luke 21:7).

In the predictions that Christ made almost two thousand years ago, He accurately portrayed the progress in the present age. In Matthew 24:4–14, He predicted at least nine distinctive features of the period: false christs (vv. 4–5); wars and rumors of wars (vv. 6–7); famines (v. 7); pestilence (v. 7 KJV); earthquakes (v. 7); many martyrs (vv. 8–10); false prophets (v. 11); increase in wickedness with love growing cold (v. 12); and worldwide preaching of the gospel of the kingdom (vv. 13–14). Luke 21:8–24 records similar prophecies.

All of these situations have been fulfilled in history. Despite advances in many areas, the world still suffers from war, famine, and pestilence. Earthquakes take on an increasingly serious role.

As the density of population increases, the earthquakes become more destructive. Scripture, of course, predicts the greatest earthquake of all time in Revelation 16:18–20, when the cities of the world will apparently be leveled shortly before the second coming of Christ. It may be true that these signs are having fulfillment in the present age with growing intensity, but ultimately they will have an even greater and more literal fulfillment in the period of the great tribulation. The three-and-a-half-year period of the great tribulation will reach its climax in the second coming of Christ.

Some problems have arisen from Matthew 24:13, where it states, "But the one who stands firm to the end will be saved" (see also Mark 13:13). A common interpretation that those who stand firm will endure to the end of the tribulation is contradicted by the fact that thousands of Christians will be martyred during the great tribulation (Rev. 7:9–17). What is meant, then, by salvation at the end of the tribulation?

This statement is best interpreted as physical deliverance, and it predicts that those who are still alive at the time of the second coming of Christ will have demonstrated their faith by standing with Christ through that period and will be delivered by Jesus, or saved, in the sense that they will be delivered from their persecutors.

Matthew 24:4–14 answers the question concerning the signs of the end and of Christ's coming and presents the general signs. This section did not deal, however, with the first question the disciples asked of when the destruction of Jerusalem would take place, as predicted by Christ in verse 2. The question is answered in Luke's gospel, though, as we'll explore next.

THE SIGN OF THE DESTRUCTION OF
JERUSALEM

> There will be great distress in the land and wrath
> against this people. (Luke 21:23)

Luke 21:20–24 addresses the sign of Jerusalem's destruction. In verse 20, Jesus stated that the sign of Jerusalem being surrounded by armies should alert the people to the fact that its destruction was imminent: "When you see Jerusalem being surrounded by armies, you will know that its desolation is near." To the extent that they would be able, they were urged to flee to the mountains and get out into the open country because it would be a terrible time of persecution for Israel (vv. 21–22). It would be especially difficult for pregnant women and nursing mothers, because God's judgment would come to the land of Israel (v. 23). Jesus predicted that many in Israel would fall by the sword or be taken as prisoners (v. 24). Jerusalem would continue to be trampled underfoot by the Gentiles until the times of the Gentiles were fulfilled (v. 24).

The times of the Gentiles began in 605 BC when Nebuchadnezzar and his armies conquered Jerusalem and took the first captives to Babylon. Since then there have been times when Israel had possession of Jerusalem temporarily but they did not have permanent possession. At the time Jesus was on earth, though God's people were in Jerusalem, the city was under the control of the Gentiles. That has continued to the present time. Even today Israel controls Jerusalem because of military support from the United States.

According to Daniel's prophecies, the times of the Gentiles will not end until the conclusion of the great tribulation, which is yet to come. The section of prophecy in Luke 21:20–24 is distinguished from the other prophecies dealing with signs of the end because Luke 21:24 has already been literally fulfilled while the other aspects of its signs, as in Matthew 24 and Mark 13, have yet to see complete fulfillment. Only the book of Luke gives the specific answer to signs of the destruction of Jerusalem.

SPECIFIC SIGNS OF THE COMING OF CHRIST

> For then there will be great distress, unequaled from the beginning of the world until now—and never to be equaled again. (Matt. 24:21)

In Matthew 24:15–26 (see also Mark 13:14–25; Luke 21:25–28), after describing the signs relating to the destruction of Jerusalem and the general signs of the progress of the present age, Jesus revealed in detail the specific signs that would be unmistakable evidence that the second coming of Christ and the end of the age were near. It is important to note that the specific signs are entirely different from the signs for the destruction of Jerusalem, though there are some similarities. In both, Israel will be in a time of trouble and tribulation. In both, those in Judea are urged to flee to the mountains. In both, Gentile power, at least at first, will be triumphant. However, the specific signs of the end of the age and the coming of Christ do not occur in connection with the destruction of Jerusalem but await the future period leading up to the second coming of Christ, which will be the definitive sign of the end.

One of the sources of confusion among interpreters of the Olivet Discourse is their attempt to find complete fulfillment of the entire Olivet Discourse in connection with the destruction of Jerusalem. This is sometimes related to the attempt to avoid specific prophecy and the tendency to avoid details in prophecy as being accurate. Actually, Christ was painting a detailed and accurate picture of the great tribulation and its effect on the inhabitants of Jerusalem. As previously pointed out, Matthew's predictions do not relate to the church age as such, the rapture of the church, or related events. Here, Matthew's gospel, reporting the prophecies of Christ, focuses on the last three and a half years leading up to the second coming. In that time there will be specific signs that will unmistakably identify the period as the time of the great tribulation.

Jesus first of all called attention to the specific sign of the appearance of "'the abomination that causes desolation' spoken of through the prophet Daniel" (Matt. 24:15). According to Daniel 9:26–27, the future world ruler, who will be in power in that period of three and a half years, will desecrate the temple and cause the sacrifices to cease. This is called "an abomination that causes desolation" because it destroys the sacred character of the sacrificial altar and the temple that will be in existence at the time. A similar event occurred in the second century BC when Antiochus Epiphanes stopped the sacrifices and desecrated the temple. This event fulfilled Daniel's prophecy, recorded in Daniel 11:31.

Matthew's account describes this event, which is yet to come, as a time when the temple will be desecrated in a similar way: "From the time that the daily sacrifice is abolished and the abomination that causes desolation is set up, there will be 1,290 days" (Dan. 12:11). This period of approximately three and a half years will be the time of the great tribulation and will climax in the second coming of Christ. Accordingly, when the temple is desecrated by the future world ruler, it will be a specific sign of the imminent coming of Christ (see also 2 Thess. 2:3–4; Rev. 13:11–15).

Just as the surrounding of Jerusalem by the Roman armies was a sign for them to flee to the mountains in Judea in AD 70, so when this temple is desecrated in the future, it will be a sign for Jews in Jerusalem to flee. It will be a very specific sign that will come on a certain day at a certain time. Jesus urged them to flee immediately when they learn of it, not even bothering to go back to their houses or to stop to get their cloaks (Matt. 24:16–18). As it was in the case when Jerusalem was destroyed, so it will be difficult for pregnant women and nursing mothers to leave home and endure the hardships of escaping Jerusalem.

Jesus also said they should pray that they will not have to leave on the Sabbath, because travel on the Sabbath day would be an obvious sign that they were fleeing, as normally they did not journey on that day (v. 20).

The initial sign of the desecration of their temple will be followed by the fearful fulfillment and the time of great trouble anticipated in the Old Testament (Jer. 30:4–7; Dan. 9:25–26). Jesus declared that "there will be great distress, unequaled from the beginning of the world until now—and never to be equaled again" (Matt. 24:21). This time of trouble will be so great that the period, if not limited to the three-and-a-half-years duration as described in

Scripture, will destroy the human race. Jesus stated, "No one would survive, but for the sake of the elect those days will be shortened" (Matt. 24:22).

All these events will be warnings that Christ is coming at the end of this period. Though people will not know the day nor the hour, they will be able to comprehend the approximate time because the length of the total period is forty-two months (Rev. 13:5). Taking all Scripture into consideration, and especially the graphic picture of the great tribulation provided in the book of Revelation, it seems that the population of the world will be decimated and only a fraction of those who enter the period will survive to the end. Jesus said, in fact, that if He did not stop the period by His second coming, there would be no human beings left on earth (Matt. 24:22).

There will also be deceitful signs and reports that Christ has already appeared: "At that time if anyone says to you, 'Look, here is the Messiah!' or, 'There he is!' do not believe it. For false messiahs and false prophets will appear and perform great signs and wonders to deceive, if possible, even the elect" (vv. 23–24; cf. Mark 13:21–23). According to Matthew 24:26, there will be reports that Jesus has appeared in the desert or has been revealed in the inner room, but believers are urged not to believe this.

The point is that the second coming of Christ will be a very visible event. Jesus described it in Matthew: "For as lightning that comes from the east is visible even in the west, so will be the coming of the Son of Man" (24:27). The second coming will be preceded by many supernatural events in the skies that are described in the book of Revelation. Jesus said, "Immediately after the distress of those days 'the sun will be darkened, and the moon will not give its light; the stars will fall from the sky, and the heavenly bodies will be shaken'" (Matt. 24:29; cf. Mark 13:24–25; Luke 21:25–26).

The final sign will be the appearance of Christ Himself in the sky in His return from heaven to the earth. Jesus said, "Then will appear the sign of the Son of Man in heaven. And then all the peoples of the earth will mourn when they see the Son of Man coming on the clouds of heaven, with power and great glory" (Matt. 24:30; cf. Mark 13:26; Luke 21:27). Revelation 19:11–16 describes the scene in greater detail.

Taken as a whole, the revelation of Matthew 24:4–31, with parallel passages in Mark and Luke, answers the questions that the disciples had raised: the first concerning the destruction of Jerusalem, which occurred in AD 70, and the second and third questions dealing with the end of the age and the coming of Christ. The event itself is preceded by the signs that Jesus described and the climax in the second coming of Christ at the beginning of His kingdom on earth.

Having answered their questions, Jesus then turned to illustrations and applications of the truths of these prophecies.

THE SECOND COMING COMPARED TO THE DAYS OF NOAH

> Keep watch, because you do not know on what day
> your Lord will come. (Matt. 24:42)

In Matthew 24:36–42, we are told that though the time of the coming of the Lord may be recognized as about to happen, details are not given in such clarity that one can determine the day or the hour.

Needless speculation concerning the time of the coming of the Lord could be avoided if this verse were taken literally. Jesus said, "About that day or hour no one knows, not even the angels in heaven, nor the Son, but only the Father" (v. 36).

Jesus, of course, was referring here to His human intelligence, which was limited, not to His divine omniscience. The time leading up to the second coming was compared to the days leading up to the flood. In the case of the flood, there were numerous signs of the approaching end, and the same will be true of the second coming. It should be noted that the signs are in relation to the second coming of Christ at the end of the tribulation, not to the rapture of the church, which has no signs and is always imminent until it occurs. Noah took more than a hundred years to build the ark. In this time, people carried on their normal activities, as Jesus mentioned (vv. 37–38). When the ark was finally finished, however, the situation suddenly changed. Now it was possible for the flood to come.

Jesus then compared the situation of the flood of Noah to the time of the second coming. He stated, "That is how it will be at the coming of the Son of Man. Two men will be in the field; one will be taken and the other left. Two women will be grinding with a hand mill; one will be taken and the other left. Therefore keep watch, because you do not know on what day your Lord will come" (Matt. 24:39–42).

Because this event is somewhat similar to the rapture in that some are taken and some are left, post-tribulationists almost universally cite this verse as proof that the rapture will occur as a part of the second coming of Christ after the tribulation. However, a careful reading of the passage yields exactly the opposite result. At the rapture of the church, those taken are saved and those who are left go through an awful period, including the great tribulation. Here, the situation is just in reverse. Those who are taken are taken in judgment, and those who are left are left to enter the millennial kingdom.

The conclusion for those living at the time of the second coming is similar to that of the time of Noah: "Therefore keep watch, because you do not know on what day your Lord will come" (Matt. 24:42). Though the passage is talking about the second coming of Christ and not the period preceding the rapture, if those living in the period before the second coming—who are able to see signs of the second coming indicating its approach—should be watching, how much more should those waiting for the rapture, which has no signs, live in constant expectation of the imminent return of Jesus for His church.

WE MUST BE WATCHFUL

You also must be ready. (Matt. 24:44)

In His great providence, God did not see fit to leave humanity in the dark about the end times. Instead, in Matthew 24:43–44, Jesus gave an example of the "watchfulness" that His believers should have while they await His return: "But understand this: If the owner of the house had known at what time of night the thief was coming, he would have kept watch and would not have let his house be broken into. So you also must be ready, because the Son of Man will come at an hour when you do not expect him."

Jesus made the application of watchfulness as would be required of the owner of a house who did not know when a thief would break in (v. 43). Not knowing the exact hour, the owner would have to watch continuously. Jesus applied this to those waiting for the second coming with the exhortation "Be ready, because the Son of Man will come at an hour when you do not expect him" (v. 44).

THE FAITHFUL WATCH AND WAIT

> Who then is the faithful and wise servant, whom
> the master has put in charge of the servants in his
> household? (Matt. 24:45)

One who is waiting for the second coming of Christ is like a servant who is put in charge of his master's house. Not knowing when his master would return, the servant was urged to be faithful (Matt. 24:45–47). If, however, the servant takes advantage of his master and abuses his fellow servants and lives the life of a drunkard, he will experience the judgment of his master when the master returns unexpectedly (vv. 48–50). Jesus stated that the unfaithful servant will be cut into pieces and placed with the hypocrites (v. 51).

The implication of this passage is that belief in the second coming of Christ is linked to belief in the first coming of Christ. If one accepts who Christ was and what He did in His first coming, the believer will also accept who Christ will be and what He will do at His second coming and, accordingly, will live in preparation.

THE PARABLE OF THE TEN VIRGINS

> Therefore keep watch, because you do not know the
> day or the hour. (Matt. 25:13)

Matthew 25:1–13 presents another illustration of the need for preparedness for the second coming. In the passage, Christ described a familiar scene in Israel—that of the bridegroom claiming his bride. The normal procedure was for a wedding to have three stages. First, the parents of the bridegroom would arrange for the marriage with the parents of the bride and would pay the dowry. This was the legal marriage.

The second stage, which often took place a year or more later, was fulfilled when the bridegroom, accompanied by his friends, would proceed from the home of the bridegroom at midnight and go to the home of the bride and claim her. The bride would know that he was coming, would be ready with her maiden friends, and would join the procession from her home to the home of the bridegroom.

The third phase of the traditional wedding was a marriage feast following this, which might take place for days and was illustrated in the wedding at Cana (John 2).

While the figure of bride and wife is used in more than one application in Scripture, typically Israel is described as the wife of the Lord, already married, and the church is pictured as a bride waiting for the coming of the Bridegroom (2 Cor. 11:2). At the rapture of the church, the Bridegroom will claim His bride and take her to heaven.

The illustration in Matthew 25 is in reference to the attendants at the wedding. Each of the ten virgins took a lamp, but only the five wise virgins took oil with their lamps. Though Scripture does not explain the spiritual meaning of these elements, frequently in the Bible the Holy Spirit is described as oil, as illustrated in the lamps burning in the tabernacle and in the temple. When the cry rang out that the bridegroom was coming (v. 6), the virgins all rose to light their lamps and meet the procession. The foolish virgins, however, had no oil at all, even in their lamps, and their wicks soon burned out. When they requested oil from the wise virgins, they were told to go buy some.

While they were out trying to make their purchase at midnight, which could have been difficult, the five wise virgins went with the procession to the home of the bridegroom, and then the door was shut (v. 10). When the five foolish virgins finally arrived, they were shut out because they were not watching for the coming of the bridegroom and his procession. As in all illustrations, the meaning of this story should not be pressed to the point where it becomes a basis for doctrine. In this case the main objective is clear. When the second coming occurs, it is going to be too late to get ready.

Though some have viewed this incident as the rapture of the church, there is really no justification for this because the context is entirely related to the second coming of Christ, and Jesus had not yet revealed any truth concerning the rapture. He could hardly, therefore, expect His disciples to understand an illustration of a truth that had not been revealed.

THE PARABLE OF THE TALENTS

Well done, good and faithful servant! (Matt. 25:23)

In Matthew 25:14–30 and Luke 19:11–27, Jesus told the parable of the talents, or bags of gold, or minas, depending on the translation. In Luke 19, while He was still in the vicinity of Jericho and on His way to Jerusalem, Jesus used the parable of the ten minas to indicate the need for working while waiting for the return of the Lord. Luke recorded how the master gave a mina to each of his ten servants and instructed them to use their minas to the best advantage while he was gone to receive appointment as king. A mina was equivalent to three months' wages. Upon his return, one servant had gained ten minas and another five, and both were commended. However, the one who hid the mina and had not done anything with it was condemned by his master because he had not taken advantage of the opportunity of making this money work for his lord.

The account in Matthew of the parable of the talents has the same illustration, somewhat changed, which Jesus used in connection with His Olivet Discourse. In the parable of the talents, the master of the house gave five talents to one servant, two to another, and one to the third and instructed the servants to work with this while he was gone. A talent was originally a weight of fifty-eight to one hundred pounds. In modern value, a single silver talent is worth in excess of two thousand dollars and a gold talent is worth in excess of thirty thousand dollars. In today's inflated prices, gold and silver are worth much more. In Jesus's time, a day's wages amounted to sixteen cents. Accordingly, these sums represented enormous values.

In the illustration that Christ used, He was referring to silver talents as illustrated in the word "money" (Matt. 25:18), which is literally silver. In the illustration, the master distributed the talents according to his estimate of their abilities. The master was gone for a long period of time, but when he returned, he called in his servants to give an account (v. 19). The five-talent man brought in an additional five talents, saying, "Lord, you delivered to me five talents; look, I have gained five more talents besides them" (v. 20 NKJV). His lord commended him: "Well done, good and faithful servant; you were faithful over a few things, I will make you ruler over many things. Enter into the joy of your lord" (v. 21 NKJV). When the two-talent man reported, he, likewise, had doubled his money and received precisely the same commendation (vv. 22–23).

The one-talent man, however, had a different report: "Lord, I knew you to be a hard man, reaping where you have not sown, and gathering where you have not scattered seed. And I was afraid, and went and hid your talent in the ground. Look, there you have what is yours" (vv. 24–25 NKJV).

The master judged his servant, saying, "You wicked and lazy servant, you knew that I reap where I have not sown, and gather where I have not scattered seed. So you ought to have deposited my money with the bankers, and at my coming I would have received back my own with interest" (vv. 26–27 NKJV). The handling of the one-talent man is one of the major points of this illustration. Why was the master so hard on his servant? The answer is that the servant indicated he had serious questions as to whether the master would return. If the master did not, the servant could keep the money and not report it as part of his master's estate. If the master returned, he would be able to reproduce the talent and could not be accused of stealing. What the unprofitable servant displayed was lack of faith in his master and a desire to have his master's money illegally.

The point is that those who reject the truth of the return of the Lord are, in effect, nullifying the fact of His first coming, as acceptance of one should lead to acceptance of the other. In the illustration the master declared, "Therefore take the talent from him, and give it to him who has ten talents. For to everyone who has, more will be given, and he will have abundance; but from him who does not have, even what he has will be taken away. And cast the unprofitable servant into the outer darkness. There will be weeping and gnashing of teeth" (vv. 28–30 NKJV).

As is brought out in 2 Peter 3:3–4, for one to question the literalness of Christ's second coming raises questions as to whether the person believed in the first coming. If Jesus is indeed the Son of God, then His coming again is both reasonable and to be expected. If He is not the Son of God, of course, He will not return. Accordingly, a lack of faith in the second coming stems from a lack of faith in the first coming. The one-talent man indicated outward profession of service to his master but did not possess real faith.

THE JUDGMENT OF THE GENTILES AT THE SECOND COMING

> When the Son of Man comes in his glory, and
> all the angels with him, he will sit on his glorious
> throne. (Matt. 25:31)

The judgment in Matthew 25:31–46 relating to the Gentiles at the time of the second coming is revealed only here in Scripture. Premillenarians interpret this judgment as determining who among the Gentiles will enter the millennial kingdom. The basis for judgment is how they treated Christ's brethren, the Jews, as a token of their faith or lack of it. Amillenarians believe that the second coming ushers in the eternal state and interpret this judgment as determining who will enter into the new heaven and the new earth. The question of whether there is a millennium after the second coming of Christ must be determined by other scriptures, as this passage in itself is not decisive.

Premillenarians contrast this judgment to several other judgments mentioned in Scripture, such as the judgment of the church (2 Cor. 5:10), the judgment of Israel, and the purging out of the rebels as a prelude to the millennial kingdom (Ezek. 20:33–38), and it is also different from the judgment of the wicked dead resurrected at the judgment of the great white throne (Rev. 20:11–15), which occurs at the end of the millennium.

The time of this judgment is clearly stated in Matthew 25:31: "When the Son of Man comes in his glory, and all the angels with him, he will sit on his glorious throne." The judgment is not of all people but of living Gentiles. The Gentiles are described as either sheep or goats, and Jews are described as brothers and sisters of Christ.

Jesus described the situation: "All the nations will be gathered before him, and he will separate the people one from another as a shepherd separates the sheep from the goats. He will put the sheep on his right and the goats on his left" (vv. 32–33). While sheep and goats look much alike, they are different breeds; and even though in ordinary life sheep and goats sometimes are in the same flock, at the proper time they could be separated.

The sheep, representing the saved, are praised for serving those in need and, inadvertently, serving Jesus. Contrarily, the goats are condemned for ignoring the needs of those around them.

Taken as a whole, this judgment fits naturally into the premillennial order of events before and after the second coming of Christ. This judgment related to the Gentiles is similar to the judgment relating to Israel (Ezek. 20:33–38). The contrast of Jews and Gentiles is a familiar one in Scripture, as Gentiles are distinguished from the Jews in their outlook and hope (see also Rom. 11:13; 15:27; 16:4; Gal. 2:12). The Gentiles are contrasted to those who are considered Jews, as noted in Romans 3:29 and 9:24.

This passage, however, has puzzled expositors because there is no preaching of the cross, there is no statement of the gospel as necessary for salvation, and all the passage speaks of is the contrast of the works of the sheep and the goats. But the answer to this problem is not a denial that salvation is based on faith and grace alone (Rom. 3:10–12, 21, 28). The passage can be seen in the light of James 2:26, which declares, "Faith without deeds is dead." What is presented here is not the grounds for salvation, but the fruit of salvation.

This judgment is also quite different from the judgment of the great white throne (Rev. 20:11–15), because there are no resurrected people here, but rather living people on earth. Further, the purpose of the judgment is to allow the righteous to enter the millennial kingdom. It should be noted that there is no resurrection related to this judgment such as would be true if it were the rapture of the church.

The passage also tends to contradict the view that the rapture occurs at the end of the tribulation at the time of the second coming. If such a rapture had taken place in the process of Christ's coming from heaven to earth and believers were caught up to meet Him, as the rapture is described, the sheep would have already been separated from the goats and no judgment like this would be necessary. After Christ's kingdom is set up on earth, there is still the mingled picture of saved and unsaved. Living Gentile believers at this judgment prove that rapture has taken place.

The Olivet Discourse takes its place among the great prophetic passages of Scripture. The judgment explains why Christ did not bring His kingdom in at His first coming: Other prophecies had to be fulfilled before the second coming could be fulfilled. Accordingly, while Christ was declared the King of Israel and the Savior of the world, He was rejected at His first coming but will return in triumph, fulfilling literally the passage in the Old Testament that describes this victory.

The disciples were ill prepared to understand this, and they, no doubt, did not understand at the time as they asked the further question in Acts 1 concerning the time that Christ would bring in His kingdom. The early church was slow to respond and understand that there would be an extensive time period between Christ's first coming and His second coming and that in it would be fulfilled God's program, unpredicted in the Old Testament—that God would call out a people, both Jews and Gentiles, to form a special body of believers for time and for eternity.

JESUS'S ASCENSION AND PROMISE OF RETURN

> After he said this, he was taken up before their very
> eyes, and a cloud hid him from their sight. (Acts 1:9)

The detailed prophecies spoken by Jesus before His death have confirming verses throughout the Old and New Testaments. Paul, Peter, and John would all write extensively about Jesus's return, but the words of Jesus in Acts 1:7–8 give us significant detail on their own.

It is worth noting that after Jesus's death, these prophecies of Jesus were confirmed by angels at the time of His ascension.

No sooner had He answered the disciples' questions than He was literally taken up from before their eyes and rose bodily from earth to the heavens. A cloud enveloped Him and hid Him from their sight. Scripture records, "They were looking intently up into the sky as he was going, when suddenly two men dressed in white stood beside them. 'Men of Galilee,' they said, 'why do you stand here looking into the sky? This same Jesus, who has been taken from you into heaven, will come back in the same way you have seen him go into heaven'" (vv. 10–11). The departure of Jesus was bodily, visible, gradual, and accompanied by a cloud. These same factors enter into His second coming as portrayed in other scriptures, including Revelation 19:11–18.

What an incredible journey through Scripture this has been! Through study of God's Word, we are witnesses of the Messiah's birth, life, death, and resurrection. We have seen how each prophecy concerning the Messiah has been fulfilled in Jesus Christ.

Having read and absorbed these prophecies, you now know your Savior more fully and completely than ever before. As believers in the death, resurrection, and ascension of Jesus Christ, we can take heart that Jesus is coming back and will have prepared a place for His followers for all time.

Armed with this knowledge of the good news, you are equipped to share this message with your friends, family, coworkers, and neighbors. I pray that this resource will serve you well as you engage in conversations that will change lives.

ORDER OF EVENTS OF BIBLE PROPHECY

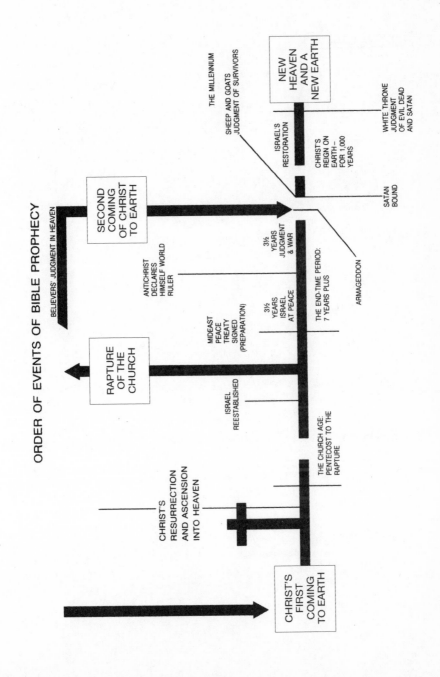

MAJOR EVENTS OF
UNFULFILLED PROPHECY

1. Rapture of the church (1 Cor. 15:51–58; 1 Thess. 4:13–18).

2. Revival of the Roman Empire; ten-nation confederacy formed (Dan. 7:7, 24; Rev. 13:1; 17:3, 12–13).

3. Rise of the Antichrist: the Middle East dictator (Dan. 7:8; Rev. 13:1–8).

4. The seven-year peace treaty with Israel: consummated seven years before the second coming of Christ (Dan. 9:27; Rev. 19:11–16).

5. Establishment of a world church (Rev. 17:1–15).

6. Russia springs a surprise attack on Israel four years before the second coming of Christ (Ezek. 38–39).

7. Peace treaty with Israel broken after three and a half years: beginning of world government, world economic system, world atheistic religion, final three and a half years before second coming of Christ (Dan. 7:23; Rev. 13:5–8, 15–17; 17:16–17).

8. Many Christians and Jews martyred who refused to worship world dictator (Rev. 7:9–17; 13:15).

9. Catastrophic divine judgments represented by seals, trumpets, and bowls poured out on the earth (Rev. 6–18).

10. World war breaks out focusing on the Middle East: Battle of Armageddon (Dan. 11:40–45; Rev. 9:13–21; 16:12–16).

11. Babylon destroyed (Rev. 18).

12. Second coming of Christ (Matt. 24:27–31; Rev. 19:11–21).

13. Judgment of wicked Jews and Gentiles (Ezek. 20:33–38; Matt. 25:31–46; Jude vv. 14–15; Rev. 19:15–21; 20:1–4).

14. Satan bound for one thousand years (Rev. 20:1–3).

15. Resurrection of tribulation saints and Old Testament saints (Dan. 12:2; Rev. 20:4).

16. Millennial kingdom begins (Rev. 20:5–6).

17. Final rebellion at the end of the millennium (Rev. 20:7–10).

18. Resurrection and final judgment of the wicked: great white throne judgment (Rev. 20:11–15).

19. Eternity begins: new heaven, new earth, New Jerusalem (Rev. 21:1–2).

PREDICTED EVENTS RELATED
TO THE CHURCH

1. Rise of liberalism and rejection of fundamental biblical doctrines permeate the professing church.
2. Communism and atheism rise as major opponents of Christianity.
3. The ecumenical movement promoting a world church organized in 1948.
4. Increased moral chaos results from departure from biblical doctrines.
5. Evidence of spiritism, the occult, and Satan worship increases.
6. The church is raptured.
7. The Holy Spirit lifts the restraint of sin.
8. "Super church" movement gains power and forms a world church.
9. World church works with the Antichrist to secure world domination.
10. Super church is destroyed by the ten leaders supporting the Antichrist to pave the way for worship of the world ruler as God.
11. Those who have come to believe in Christ as Savior since the rapture suffer persecution because they refuse to worship the world ruler.
12. Second coming of Christ occurs, and remaining Christians in the world are rescued and enter the millennial kingdom.
13. After the millennium the church is placed in the New Jerusalem on the new earth.

APPEARANCES OF JESUS
AFTER THE RESURRECTION

1. To Mary Magdalene when she returned to the tomb (John 20:11–17; cf. Mark 16:9–11).

2. To the other women as they were returning to the tomb a second time (Matt. 28:9–10).

3. To Peter in the afternoon of resurrection day (Luke 24:34; 1 Cor. 15:5).

4. To the disciples on the road to Emmaus (Mark 16:12–13; Luke 24:13–35).

5. To the ten disciples (Mark 16:14; Luke 24:36–43; John 20:19–23).

6. To the eleven disciples a week after His resurrection, Thomas being present (John 20:26–29).

7. To the seven disciples by the Sea of Galilee (John 21:1–23).

8. To five hundred people as reported by Paul (1 Cor. 15:6).

9. To James, the Lord's brother (1 Cor. 15:7).

10. To the eleven disciples on a mountain in Galilee (Matt. 28:16–20; Mark 16:15–18).

11. At the time of His ascension from the Mount of Olives (Luke 24:44–53; Acts 1:3–9).

12. To Stephen at the time of his martyrdom (Acts 7:55–56).

13. To Paul on the road to Damascus (Acts 9:3–6; 22:6–11; 26:13–18).

14. To Paul in Arabia (Gal. 1:12, 17).

15. To Paul in the temple (Acts 22:17–21).

16. To Paul in the prison in Caesarea (Acts 23:11).

17. To the apostle John at the beginning of the revelation given to him (Rev. 1:12–20).

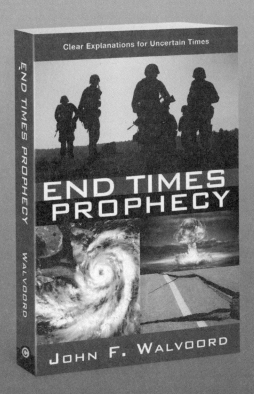

BONUS CONTENT

CHAPTERS 1–2 FROM ...

END TIMES PROPHECY

Ancient Wisdom for Uncertain Times

JOHN F. WALVOORD

David C Cook®

transforming lives together

END TIMES PROPHECY
Published by David C Cook
4050 Lee Vance View
Colorado Springs, CO 80918 U.S.A.

David C Cook Distribution Canada
55 Woodslee Avenue, Paris, Ontario, Canada N3L 3E5

David C Cook U.K., Kingsway Communications
Eastbourne, East Sussex BN23 6NT, England

The graphic circle C logo is a registered trademark of David C Cook.

LCCN 2015960922
ISBN 978-1-4347-0991-2
eISBN 978-0-7814-1432-6

© 2016 John F. Walvoord
Material adapted from *Every Prophecy of the Bible* (formerly titled
Prophecy Knowledge Handbook) © 1990, 2011 John F. Walvoord,
published by David C Cook, ISBN 978-1-4347-0386-6.

The Team: Tim Peterson, Keith Wall, Amy Konyndyk,
Nick Lee, Jack Campbell, Susan Murdock
Cover Design: Jon Middel
Cover Photo: Thinkstock

Printed in the United States of America
First Edition 2016

1 2 3 4 5 6 7 8 9 10

012816

CONTENTS

AN END TIMES TIMELINE

Because there is so much confusion and disagreement about the end times, even among Christians, this chapter is meant to serve as an overview—a timeline that will help you visualize the major events of unfulfilled prophecy. In this chapter, you will see summaries of occurrences from the rapture through Christ's final judgment and the beginning of the eternal heavenly reign. Each of these events will be dealt with at more length throughout the rest of the book.

1. Rapture of the Church (1 Cor. 15:51–58; 1 Thess. 4:13–18)

The first concrete event of the end times is the rapture, the moment when Jesus Christ takes up all believers to be with Him in heaven, before the turmoil and persecution of the tribulation begins.

> Brothers and sisters, we do not want you to be uninformed about those who sleep in death, so that you do not grieve like the rest of mankind, who have no hope.... For the Lord himself will come down from heaven, with a loud command, with the voice of the archangel and with the trumpet call of

> God, and the dead in Christ will rise first. After
> that, we who are still alive and are left will be caught
> up together with them in the clouds to meet the
> Lord in the air. And so we will be with the Lord
> forever. (1 Thess. 4:13, 16–17)

This revelation was introduced as truth that is "according to
the Lord's word" (v. 15), given to the apostle Paul by special revelation. Though Jesus introduced the doctrine of the rapture in John
14:1–3, there was no exposition of it while He was still on earth.
This revelation, given to Paul to pass on to the Thessalonian church,
becomes an important additional message concerning the nature of
the rapture.

2. Revival of the Roman Empire; Ten-Nation Confederacy Formed (Dan. 7:7, 24; Rev. 13:1; 17:3, 12–13)

Specific political realities have also been predicted in Scripture.
Alliances and wars will happen according to prophecy.

> After that, in my vision at night I looked, and there
> before me was a fourth beast—terrifying and fright-
> ening and very powerful. It had large iron teeth;
> it crushed and devoured its victims and trampled
> underfoot whatever was left. It was different from
> all the former beasts, and it had ten horns....
>
> The ten horns are ten kings who will come
> from this kingdom. After them another king will
> arise, different from the earlier ones. (Dan. 7:7, 24)

In Daniel's vision, the four beasts represented four kingdoms. The fourth kingdom was not named but was historically fulfilled by the Roman Empire. As described in verse 7, it crushed and devoured the countries it conquered. The ten horns represented a future Roman Empire that will reappear in the end times.

3. Rise of the Antichrist: The Middle East Dictator (Dan. 7:8; Rev. 13:1–8)

The leader of this new Roman Empire is also predicted. Daniel's beastly metaphor continues:

> There before me was another horn, a little one,
> which came up among them; and three of the first
> horns were uprooted before it. This horn had eyes
> like the eyes of a human being and a mouth that
> spoke boastfully. (Dan. 7:8)

The Antichrist will be known by his boastful arrogance and for setting himself up against God's authority.

4. The Seven-Year Peace Treaty with Israel: Consummated Seven Years before the Second Coming of Christ (Dan. 9:27; Rev. 19:11–16)

This Antichrist will deal duplicitously with God's chosen nation, Israel.

> He will confirm a covenant with many for one "seven."
> In the middle of the "seven" he will put an end to sac-
> rifice and offering. And at the temple he will set up an

> abomination that causes desolation, until the end that
> is decreed is poured out on him. (Dan. 9:27)

This treaty will initially be seen as a positive mark of this world ruler's leadership. The leader will be charismatic and popular, hence his worldwide sway and influence.

5. Establishment of a World Church (Rev. 17:1–15)

The significant events won't be marked only by secular politics. There will be effects in the religious sphere as well.

> One of the seven angels who had the seven bowls
> came and said to me, "Come, I will show you the
> punishment of the great prostitute, who sits by
> many waters." ...
> The name written on her forehead was a mystery:
> Babylon the Great, the Mother of Prostitutes and of
> the Abominations of the Earth. (Rev. 17:1, 5)

Since true believers have already been raptured, those left on earth merely professed faith in Jesus but were not truly part of the church invisible. Those who remain—whatever they claim—will be part of the remnants of a universal "Babylonian" church. This church will dominate the world politically and religiously up to the midpoint of the last seven years before Christ's second coming.

6. Russia Springs a Surprise Attack on Israel Four Years before the Second Coming of Christ (Ezek. 38–39)

While the entire tribulation is marked by "wars and rumors of wars," things will now get specific.

> Son of man, set your face against Gog, of the land of Magog, the chief prince of Meshek and Tubal [or Rosh]....
>
> Get ready; be prepared, you and all the hordes gathered about you, and take command of them. After many days you will be called to arms. In future years you will invade a land that has recovered from war, whose people were gathered from many nations to the mountains of Israel, which had long been desolate. They had been brought out from the nations, and now all of them live in safety. (Ezek. 38:2, 7–8)

The ancient princes listed in Ezekiel 38 correspond with modern-day Russia. But there will be an alliance of several groups and nations that suddenly wage war against Israel.

7. Peace Treaty with Israel Broken after Three and a Half Years: Beginning of World Government, World Economic System, World Atheistic Religion, Final Three and a Half Years before the Second Coming of Christ (Dan. 7:23; Rev. 13:5–8, 15–17; 17:16–17)
The Antichrist's predicted and inevitable betrayal of Israel will occur halfway through the seven-year tribulation.

> [The beast] was given power to wage war against God's holy people and to conquer them. And it was

> given authority over every tribe, people, language
> and nation. All inhabitants of the earth will wor-
> ship the beast. (Rev. 13:7–8)

Using the power and alliances that he has built in the preceding three and a half years, the charismatic leader will consolidate his
authority over all the nations. His rule will not be limited just to
politics; he will take over the economy and religion as well.

8. Many Christians and Jews Who Refused to Worship the World Dictator Are Martyred (Rev. 7:9–17; 13:15)

Throughout this political and military upheaval, some people will
be persuaded by the events to worship Christ. These, sadly, who
were not believers in time to be raptured, will be persecuted and
even killed for following the one true faith instead of the Antichrist's
Babylonian religion.

> The second beast was given power to give breath
> to the image of the first beast, so that the image
> could speak and cause all who refused to worship
> the image to be killed. (Rev. 13:15)

9. Catastrophic Divine Judgments Represented by Seals, Trumpets, and Bowls Poured Out on the Earth (Rev. 6–18)

As bad as the tribulation has been up to this point, it still has room
to get worse. God will unleash cosmic catastrophes on the entire
earth.

> There was a great earthquake. The sun turned black like sackcloth made of goat hair, the whole moon turned blood red, and the stars in the sky fell to earth, as figs drop from a fig tree when shaken by a strong wind. The heavens receded like a scroll being rolled up, and every mountain and island was removed from its place. (Rev. 6:12–14)

The earth will experience physical, geological consequences of God's wrath and judgment.

10. World War Breaks Out Focusing on the Middle East: Battle of Armageddon (Dan. 11:40–45; Rev. 9:13–21; 16:12–16)

While most will quake in fear at the physical destruction around them, the Antichrist will take it as an opportunity to crush all who are not in thrall to him.

> He will invade many countries and sweep through them like a flood. He will also invade the Beautiful Land. Many countries will fall. (Dan. 11:40–41)

11. Babylon Destroyed (Rev. 18)

For all his plotting, and his political and military might, the Antichrist is still under the sovereign plan of God. All his striving and grasping for authority will ultimately serve only to be the final sign of Jesus Christ's second coming. The capital of his kingdom, the metaphorical Babylon, will be destroyed.

Then a mighty angel picked up a boulder the size of a large millstone and threw it into the sea, and said:

"With such violence
    the great city of Babylon will be thrown down,
    never to be found again." (Rev. 18:21)

12. Second Coming of Christ (Matt. 24:27–31; Rev. 19:11–21)

Finally! The blessed and awaited event will happen. Christ will come down in His full power and authority.

Then will appear the sign of the Son of Man in heaven. And then all the peoples of the earth will mourn when they see the Son of Man coming on the clouds of heaven, with power and great glory. And he will send his angels with a loud trumpet call, and they will gather his elect from the four winds, from one end of the heavens to the other. (Matt. 24:30–31)

The earth will "mourn" because by this time all of Christ's believers will have been either raptured or martyred. The people left on earth will be those who have rejected Christ. This will lead to the next event.

13. Judgment of Wicked Jews and Gentiles (Ezek. 20:33–38; Matt. 25:31–46; Jude vv. 14–15; Rev. 19:15–21; 20:1–4)

This is not the ultimate judgment of believers. This is an earthly judgment of the wicked, preliminary to Christ's "great white throne judgment" of the living and the dead.

> See, the Lord is coming with thousands upon thousands of his holy ones to judge everyone, and to convict all of them of all the ungodly acts they have committed in their ungodliness, and of all the defiant words ungodly sinners have spoken against him. (Jude vv. 14–15)

14. Satan Bound for One Thousand Years (Rev. 20:1–3)

When Christ comes at the end of the tribulation, He will judge the living who have survived the catastrophes. He will also judge Satan himself, keeping him out of trouble during Christ's millennial kingdom.

> And I saw an angel coming down out of heaven, having the key to the Abyss and holding in his hand a great chain. He seized the dragon, that ancient serpent, who is the devil, or Satan, and bound him for a thousand years. (Rev. 20:1–2)

15. Resurrection of Tribulation Saints and Old Testament Saints (Dan. 12:2; Rev. 20:4)

With all the wicked (people and demons) out of the way, Christ will now resurrect those faithful who had died before this time.

> Multitudes who sleep in the dust of the earth will
> awake: some to everlasting life, others to shame and
> everlasting contempt. (Dan. 12:2)

16. Millennial Kingdom Begins (Rev. 20:5–6)

Together with Christ, all the resurrected faithful will live and rule with their Lord in God's predicted glorious kingdom. This will be a time of peace, righteousness, and spiritual prosperity for all believers.

> Blessed and holy are those who share in the first resur-
> rection. The second death has no power over them,
> but they will be priests of God and of Christ and will
> reign with him for a thousand years. (Rev. 20:6)

17. Final Rebellion at the End of the Millennium (Rev. 20:7–10)

After one thousand years of peace, Satan will have one final opportunity to work deception on God's people.

> When the thousand years are over, Satan will
> be released from his prison and will go out to
> deceive the nations in the four corners of the
> earth—Gog and Magog—and to gather them for
> battle. (Rev. 20:7–8)

This will be the last earthly battle. And while Satan might think this his final chance for victory, in truth it will only be the final step before Christ's ultimate judgment and the beginning of His eternal reign in heaven.

18. Resurrection and Final Judgment of the Wicked: Great White Throne Judgment (Rev. 20:11–15)

At this time, all beings will be judged—human and demon, believers and unbelievers, living and dead. All will be under the authority of Christ on His heavenly throne.

> Then I saw a great white throne and him who was seated on it. The earth and the heavens fled from his presence, and there was no place for them. And I saw the dead, great and small, standing before the throne, and books were opened. Another book was opened, which is the book of life. The dead were judged according to what they had done as recorded in the books. (Rev. 20:11–12)

This is the last moment for the "old heaven" and the "old earth." All things that have been will now pass away.

19. Eternity Begins: New Heaven, New Earth, New Jerusalem (Rev. 21:1–4)

The eternal life that Jesus promised us will finally begin. And in this new place there will be no sadness or grief.

> Then I saw "a new heaven and a new earth," for the first heaven and the first earth had passed away, and there was no longer any sea. I saw the Holy City, the new Jerusalem, coming down out of heaven from God, prepared as a bride beautifully dressed

for her husband. And I heard a loud voice from the throne saying, "Look! God's dwelling place is now among the people, and he will dwell with them. They will be his people, and God himself will be with them and be their God." (Rev. 21:1–3)

We will finally be restored to our original, unbroken relationship with God that we had in the garden of Eden. We will walk with Him, and we will never be separated from our God again.

As you can see, many significant events transpire. But remember, these prophecies were meant not to confuse God's believers but to give us hope and secure knowledge of God's promises. May these prophecies encourage you as you learn more about them in the pages ahead.

2

WHAT IS THE RAPTURE?

When you hear the word *rapture*, what comes to mind? There is perhaps no other word in Scripture shrouded in such mystery. Beliefs regarding the rapture differ from church to church, believer to believer. But it doesn't have to be a confusing or intimidating topic. In fact, having a sound understanding of the rapture can enhance one's faith and strengthen one's relationship with God.

The original meaning of the word *rapture* is "great joy." Indeed, the rapture will be a great joy to those found in Christ. Hollywood portrayals of the rapture focus on the bewilderment of unbelievers when multitudes of people suddenly disappear. But that's an incomplete picture of the event. The passages in this chapter will shed light on what the Bible tells us about this mysterious yet hopeful event of the end times.

THE DAY OF CHRIST

... on the day of Christ. (Phil. 2:16)

The day of Christ in Scripture needs to be distinguished from the more common expression "the day of the Lord." The day of the

Lord normally has in view an extended period of time in which God deals in direct judgment on the world. This is developed, for instance, in 1 Thessalonians 5. The day of Christ, which is referred to with various wordings, refers to the rapture itself and the immediate results of the rapture and, therefore, does not deal with judgment on the world.

In 1 Corinthians 1:7–8, Paul stated, "Therefore you do not lack any spiritual gift as you eagerly wait for our Lord Jesus Christ to be revealed. He will also keep you firm to the end, so that you will be blameless on the day of our Lord Jesus Christ."

The reference in 1 Corinthians 5:5 is in the context of the rapture of the church, though the expression used is the more common phrase "the day of the Lord." Philippians 1:6 uses "the day of Christ Jesus," and Philippians 1:10 says "the day of Christ." In Philippians 2:16, the familiar expression "the day of Christ" again is used in reference to the rapture.

Though the varied wording does not in itself specify what day is in view, the context of these references indicates a connection to the rapture rather than to the day of the Lord, which will begin at the rapture of the church and extend through the tribulation and through the millennial kingdom, climaxing at the end of the millennium. Paul had confidence that God, who had begun a good work in the Philippian church, would continue His work until the day of the rapture and that the Philippian church would be found "pure and blameless for the day of Christ" (1:10). As the rapture of the church removes the church from the world, it will be followed immediately by the judgment seat of Christ in heaven when the works of believers will be evaluated and rewarded.

THE TIMING OF THE RAPTURE

> For God did not appoint us to suffer wrath but to
> receive salvation through our Lord Jesus Christ.
> (1 Thess. 5:9)

The day of the Lord will begin as a time period at the rapture, but its major events will not occur immediately. The ten-nation kingdom must be formed in the final seven years before the second coming will begin. Because the day of the Lord will start at the time of the rapture, the two events are linked as both beginning without warning and coming without a specific sign. However, once the day of the Lord begins, as it will after the rapture, and as time progresses, there will be obvious signs that the world is in the day of the Lord and in the period leading up to the second coming, just as there will be obvious evidences that the millennial kingdom has begun after the second coming. As the rapture must precede the signs, it necessarily must occur when the day of the Lord begins. (For further discussion, see 2 Thessalonians 2.)

One of the important signs of the day of the Lord is the fact that the people will be saying, "Peace and safety," when, as a matter of fact, "destruction will come on them suddenly, as labor pains on a pregnant woman, and they will not escape" (1 Thess. 5:3). The interpretation that this is the period between the rapture and the second coming seems most convincing. According to Daniel 9:27, there will be a seven-year period leading up to the second coming of Christ. The first half of this period will be a time when a covenant of peace will be made with Israel, as indicated in Daniel 9:27. During this period, people will hail peace as having been achieved, as mentioned in 1 Thessalonians 5:3. Then suddenly the great tribulation will begin and they will not escape its judgment. The world-shaking judgments that precede the second coming are described graphically in Revelation 6–18.

Because Christians are forewarned that the day of the Lord is coming, they should not be surprised and should live in the light of God's divine revelation. "But you, brothers and sisters, are not in darkness so that this day should surprise you like a thief. You are all children of the light and children of the day. We do not belong to the night or to the darkness" (1 Thess. 5:4–5). The day of the Lord is pictured here as a time of night for the world because it is a time of judgment, in contrast to the Christian's day, which is a time of light. The Christian's day will be climaxed by the rapture; the day for the wicked will begin at that time, and the judgments related to the day of the Lord will take place according to the time sequence of this period, with the great judgments occurring in the great tribulation and climaxing in the second coming. (Further descriptions of the day of the Lord are found in Isaiah 13:9–11 and Zephaniah 1:14–18; 3:4–15.)

As for the destinies of those who will be saved at the time of the rapture and those who are not brought out, "God did not appoint us to suffer wrath but to receive salvation through our Lord Jesus Christ" (1 Thess. 5:9). For Christians, their appointment is the rapture; for the unsaved, their appointment is the day of the Lord.

Paul realized that some Christians would have died before the rapture and that others would still be living. Accordingly, he said of Christ, "He died for us so that, whether we are awake or asleep, we may live together with him" (1 Thess. 5:10). By "awake," he was referring to Christians being still alive in the world; by "asleep," to the fact that Christians have died and their bodies will be "sleeping" in the grave though their souls are in heaven. His conclusion here, as in the other prophetic truths revealed in 1 Thessalonians, was a practical one: "Therefore encourage one another and build each other up, just as in fact you are doing" (v. 11).

THE FIRST PROMISE OF THE RAPTURE

> Do not let your hearts be troubled. You believe in God; believe also in me. My Father's house has many rooms; if that were not so, would I have told you that I am going there to prepare a place for you? And if I go and prepare a place for you, I will come back and take you to be with me that you also may be where I am. (John 14:1–3)

When they first heard that Jesus was going away, the apostles reacted immediately with fear and concern. With this comforting promise, Jesus described the rapture to His closest followers to assuage their fears. In light of His departure, Jesus promised them that He would return.

This was an entirely new revelation to be contrasted to Christ's earlier revelation concerning His second coming to judge the world. The newly mentioned purpose was to remove them from the world and take them to the Father's house, which clearly refers to heaven, where Jesus has gone before to prepare a place for those who believe in Him. This is the first reference in the New Testament to what Paul later referred to as the rapture of the church, as you will see in the next two prophecies.

THE REVEALING OF THE RAPTURE

> Brothers and sisters, we do not want you to be uninformed about those who sleep in death, so that you do not grieve like the rest of mankind, who have no hope.... For the Lord himself will come down from heaven, with a loud command, with the voice of the archangel and with the trumpet call of God, and the dead in Christ will rise first. After that, we who are still alive and are left will be caught up together with them in the clouds to meet the Lord in the air. And so we will be with the Lord forever. (1 Thess. 4:13, 16–17)

Taking its place alongside 1 Corinthians 15:51–58, the 1 Thessalonians 4:13–18 passage becomes one of the crucial revelations in regard to the rapture of the church. Though the Old Testament and the Synoptic Gospels reveal much concerning the second coming of Christ, the specific revelation concerning Christ's coming to take His church out of the world, both living and dead, was not revealed until John 14:1–3, the night before His crucifixion. Because the apostles at that time did not understand the difference between the first and second comings of Christ, they could hardly be instructed in the difference between the rapture of the church and Christ's second coming to judge and rule over the earth. A careful study of the passage in 1 Thessalonians 4 will do much to set the matter in its proper biblical revelation.

Unlike passages that deal with the second coming of Christ and trace the tremendous world-shaking events that will take place in the years preceding it, the rapture of the church is always presented as the next event and, as such, one that is not dependent on immediate preceding events. The rapture of the church, defined in 1 Thessalonians 4:17 as being "caught up together with them in the clouds to meet the Lord in the air," is a wonderful truth designed especially to encourage Christians.

Paul stated that he did not want the Thessalonians to be uninformed or ignorant concerning Christians who had died. As such, they were not to grieve for them as the world did, having no hope. In this passage, as in all scriptures, the sad lot of those who leave this world without faith in Christ is described in absolute terms of having "no hope" (v. 13). Only in Christ can one have hope of life to come in heaven.

Verse 14 states the nature of their faith in Christ that prompts them to believe that they will be ready when Christ comes: "We believe that Jesus died and rose again, and so we believe that God will bring with Jesus those who have fallen asleep in him."

If we can accept the supernatural event of Christ's dying for sin and rising from the grave, we can also believe in the future rapture of the church. This is defined as faith "that God will bring with Jesus those who have fallen asleep in him" (v. 14). At the rapture, believers are caught up to heaven. At the second coming, believers remain on earth. Accordingly, the event that Paul was describing here is quite different from the second coming of Christ as it is normally defined.

In what sense will Jesus bring with Him those who have fallen asleep? This refers to Christians who have died, and the expression of falling asleep is used to emphasize the fact that their deaths are temporary. When Christians die, their souls go immediately to heaven (2 Cor. 5:6–8). Paul declared that Jesus would bring with Him the souls of those who have fallen asleep. The purpose is brought out for this in the next verses: Jesus will cause their bodies to be raised from the dead and their souls will reenter their bodies (1 Thess. 4:15–16).

The actual sequence of events was described by Paul:

> According to the Lord's word, we tell you that we who are still alive, who are left until the coming of the Lord, will certainly not precede those who have fallen asleep. For the Lord himself will come down from heaven, with a loud command, with the voice of the archangel and with the trumpet call of God, and the dead in Christ will rise first. After that, we who are still alive and are left will be caught up together with them in the clouds to meet the Lord in the air. And so we will be with the Lord forever. (1 Thess. 4:15–17)

One question the Thessalonians seemed to face was this: If the Lord came for the living, would they have to wait before they could see those who were resurrected from the dead? Paul addressed this thought when he stated, "We who are still alive, who are left until the coming of the Lord, will certainly not precede those who have fallen asleep" (1 Thess. 4:15). In verse 16, the sequence of events is described. The Lord Jesus Himself will come down from heaven; that is, there will be a bodily return to earth. Jesus will utter a loud command related to the resurrection of the dead and the translation of the living. This will be accompanied by the voice of the archangel, which will be followed by the trumpet call of God. When this sounds, the event will take place. Christians who have died will rise first. Then Christians still living will be translated into bodies suited for heaven and "caught up together with them in the clouds to meet the Lord in the air" (v. 17).

For all practical purposes, these events will take place at the same time. Those living on earth who are translated will not have to wait for the resurrection of Christians who have died because those who are deceased will be resurrected a moment before. In expressing the thought that those who "are left will be caught up together with them in the clouds" (v. 17), Paul was revealing the essential character of the rapture, which is a snatching up or a bodily lifting up of those on earth, whether living or resurrected; their meeting the Lord in the air; and then their triumphant return to heaven. The event is described as being "with the Lord forever" (v. 17).

This is in keeping with the original revelation of the rapture in John 14:1–3, in which Christ informed His disciples that He would return for them to take them to the Father's house in heaven. They will remain in heaven until the great events in the period preceding the second coming of Christ take place, and the church in heaven will participate in the grand procession described in Revelation 19 of Christ's return to earth to set up His earthly kingdom.

The mention of clouds (1 Thess. 4:17) is taken by some to be literal clouds, as was true of Christ's ascension (Acts 1:9). Some believe the great number of those raptured will resemble a cloud, similar to the reference of Hebrews 12:1. The glorious prospect is that once this takes place, there will be no more separations between Christ and His church.

The locale of the church's future is not permanent, as they will be in heaven during the time preceding the second coming. They will be on earth during the millennial kingdom and then will inhabit the new heaven and new earth in eternity. In each of these situations, they will be with Christ in keeping with the symbolism of their marriage to Him as the heavenly Bridegroom.

Most significant in this passage is the fact that there are no preceding events, that is, no world-shaking events described as leading up to this event. In fact, the church down through the centuries expected the rapture to happen at any time, a hope that continues today. By contrast, the second coming of Christ will be preceded by divine judgments on the world and followed by the establishing of Christ's earthly kingdom. No mention is made of that here, but the emphasis is placed on the wonderful fellowship Christians will enjoy with the Savior. The wonderful hope of the rapture of the church is a source of constant encouragement to those who put their trust in Him and are looking forward to His coming.

THE MYSTERY OF THE RAPTURE

We will not all sleep, but we will all be changed—
in a flash, in the twinkling of an eye, at the last

trumpet. For the trumpet will sound, the dead will be raised imperishable, and we will be changed. For the perishable must clothe itself with the imperishable, and the mortal with immortality. When the perishable has been clothed with the imperishable, and the mortal with immortality, then the saying that is written will come true: "Death has been swallowed up in victory." (1 Cor. 15:51–54)

As is brought out in the doctrine of the rapture (1 Thess. 4:14–17), not only will living Christians be caught up to heaven without dying, but those Christians who have died will also be resurrected. Both will receive new bodies that are suited for heaven. As Paul stated, they will be imperishable and will never be subject to decay, and they will be immortal, not subject to death (1 Cor. 15:53). They will also be free from sin and be the objects of God's grace and blessing throughout eternity.

The rapture of the church will mark a victory over death and the grave. Paul said, "Death has been swallowed up in victory. 'Where, O death, is your victory? Where, O death, is your sting?'" (1 Cor. 15:54–55). Paul was quoting from Isaiah 25:8, which states that God will "swallow up death forever," and from Hosea 13:14, in which God said, "I will deliver this people from the power of the grave; I will redeem them from death. Where, O death, are your plagues? Where, O grave, is your destruction?" This doctrine is stated with greater clarity in the New Testament as Paul traced the victory through Jesus Christ: "But thanks be to God! He gives us the victory through our Lord Jesus Christ" (1 Cor. 15:57).

In light of the great doctrine of the resurrection and the imminent hope of the Lord's return, believers are exhorted to make the most of their remaining time on earth. Paul continued, "Therefore, my dear brothers and sisters, stand firm. Let nothing move you. Always give yourselves fully to the work of the Lord, because you know that your labor in the Lord is not in vain" (v. 58). Believers should stand firm because we are standing on the rock Christ Jesus and on the sure promises of God. We should not allow the vicissitudes of life and the sorrows and burdens that come to move us away from confidence in God. While living out our lives on earth, we are to engage in the work of the Lord always as to time and fully as to extent, because we know that following this life at the judgment seat of Christ we will be rewarded and our "labor in the Lord is not in vain" (v. 58). This passage (1 Cor. 15:51–58) dealing with the rapture of the church coupled with Paul's earlier revelation of the Thessalonians (1 Thess. 4:14–17) constitute the principal scriptures on this great truth of the Lord's coming and the bright hope that it could be soon.

CHRIST APPEARS TO BELIEVERS FIRST

> In the sight of God, who gives life to everything, and of Christ Jesus …, I charge you to keep this command without spot or blame until the appearing of our Lord Jesus Christ, which God will bring about in his own time. (1 Tim. 6:13–15)

In connection with Paul's charge to Timothy to obey God and to have his testimony "without spot or blame" (v. 14), Paul viewed the Lord Jesus Christ as the final judge of this situation, who will judge Timothy at the time of His coming. Though Christ will not appear to the entire world until the time of His second coming, He obviously will appear to those who are raptured in the period before these end time events. At that time, Timothy's exemplary life will be evaluated. The Christian life has its completion at the time of Christ's coming.

THE HOPE OF BEING BROUGHT SAFELY TO CHRIST'S HEAVENLY KINGDOM

> For the grace of God … teaches us to say "No" to ungodliness and worldly passions, and to live self-controlled, upright and godly lives in this present age, while we wait for the blessed hope—the appearing of the glory of our great God and Savior, Jesus Christ, who gave himself for us to redeem us from all wickedness and to purify for himself a people that are his very own, eager to do what is good. (Titus 2:11–14)

In appealing to Titus, Paul stated that the gospel of salvation "teaches us to say 'No' to ungodliness and worldly passions, and to live self-controlled, upright and godly lives in this present age" (v. 12). As we live our lives in this world, we have a wonderful hope. As Paul expressed it, "While we wait for the blessed hope—the appearing of the glory of our great God and Savior, Jesus Christ" (v. 13). This hope, obviously, related to the rapture of the church rather than the second coming of Christ to set up His kingdom, but the question has been raised as to why it is described as "the appearing of the glory."

At His second coming, Jesus will appear in a glorious event described in Revelation 19:11–16, an event that all the world will see (1:7). On the other hand, the rapture of the church is never described as visible to the world. The question therefore remains: How can the rapture be described as a glorious event, as an event that reveals the glory of God? The answer is quite simple.

While the world will not see the glory of Christ at the time of the rapture, as they will at the time of the second coming, at the rapture Christians will behold Him in His glory and to them it will be a glorious appearing. As stated in 1 John 3:2, "What we will be has not yet been made known. But we know that when Christ appears, we shall be like him, for we shall see him as he is."

Christians will necessarily need to be changed into bodies that are sinless in order to behold the Lord in His holy glory. The fact that we will "see him as he is" demonstrates that Christians will be transformed, which will make it possible for them to see Him in His glory.

CHRIST IS COMING TO RESCUE YOU

> In just a little while,
>> he who is coming will come
>> and will not delay. (Heb. 10:37)

As the Christian looks forward to relief from the present persecutions and difficulties, the promise is given, "In just a little while, he who is coming will come and will not delay" (v. 37). The reference, no doubt, is to the rapture of the church when every Christian, whether living or dead, will be caught up with the Lord. Necessarily, this will end the conflicts and problems of this life and constitute a part of the certain hope of Christians as we look to God to solve our problems.

CHRIST IS COMING SOON. TAKE HOPE!

> The end of all things is near. Therefore be alert and
> of sober mind so that you may pray. (1 Pet. 4:7)

In this brief statement, the fact that life will not go on forever should be an encouragement to Christians who are going through deep trouble. A Christian's pilgrimage on earth is temporary and soon may be cut short by the rapture of the church. This should serve as a stimulus to faithful service and endurance where persecutions and trials may be the lot of an individual Christian.

As these last few prophecies have shown us, the rapture is not meant to scare or cause us to lose sleep. Instead, the rapture offers hope. We may be suffering in this present world of brokenness and sin, but our Lord will not abandon us. He is coming back to take us away from this world, and we will truly experience the "great joy" that the word *rapture* originally intended.